CHAOS & LOVE

Thomas Bredsdorff

CHAOS & LOVE

The Philosophy of the Icelandic Family Sagas

Translated from Danish by
John Tucker

Museum Tusculanum Press
University of Copenhagen
2001

Thomas Bredsdorff: Chaos and Love
© Museum Tusculanum Press & the author, 2001
Danish title: *Kaos og kærlighed* (Copenhagen, 1971, 1995),
translated by John Tucker
Copy editors: Marianne Alenius and Signe Juul Hansen
Cover design: Veronique van der Neut
Photo on front cover, "Hekla in eruption" (detail): Sigurjón Sindrason
Photo of the author on back cover: Lars Hansen
Composition: Ole Klitgaard (the book is set in Bembo)
Printed in Denmark by Narayana Press, Gylling
ISBN 87 7289 570 5

Published with the support from
Politiken Fonden
Unibank-fonden

MUSEUM TUSCULANUM PRESS
University of Copenhagen
Njalsgade 92
DK-2300 Copenhagen S
www.mtp.dk

CONTENTS

PREFACE 7

1. THE SECOND PATTERN 13
   Thorolf's Saga *13*
   Egil Skallagrimsson's Saga *23*
   Laxdæla Saga *35*

2. FORERUNNERS 51
   Kormak's Saga, Bjorn's Saga, Eyrbyggja Saga *51*

3. THE SECOND PATTERN: BETWEEN TWO SOCIETIES *60*
   Gisli Sursson's Saga *59*

4. THE ICELANDIC MYTH 73
   Njal's Saga *72*

5. POST-CLASSICAL SAGAS 87
   Hrafnkel's Saga *86*
   Grettir's Saga *94*

6. THE SECOND PATTERN AND THE TIME OF THE
   SAGA OF ICELANDERS 102
   The Times *101*
   Histories and Two Historians *109*
   The Conceptual Universe of the Icelandic Sagas *117*
   Continuations *126*

7. BOOKS ON THE SAGAS OF ICELANDERS 130

SELECT BIBLIOGRAPHY 145

POSTSCRIPT TO THE ENGLISH EDITION 149

PREFACE

As starting point one might choose the poet and critic Carsten Hauch, who gave a series of lectures on the sagas of Icelanders at the University of Copenhagen in 1848-49.

Hauch argued that where an *artistic structure* or *design* might be discerned in a narrative – in the weaving together of events and deeds – the working of an *artistic spirit* could safely be inferred (Hauch 1855, 423). Such was the case in *Njal's Saga*, he maintained, and in other sagas of Icelanders too. Hence, he asserted, they were the work of authors.

This was new. No one disputed that other works included in the compass of Icelandic saga literature were fabricated – "lying sagas" as some called the old romantic sagas, a name leaving no doubt as to what one is dealing with. But not the sagas of Icelanders, which only a few years earlier had been published under the title: *Historical* Narratives Concerning the Icelanders' Deeds at Home and Abroad.

Certainly it was well understood already at the time that these narratives could scarcely have been written down less than one or two hundred years after the events they related. But at the same time scholars had come to believe that events had been given narrative form immediately and then passed down unchanged from generation to generation as a kind of "free prose," until writing arrived in Iceland and they were committed to parchment.

But since the events related in the stories were supposed to have taken place in the period 930-1030, and the business of writing cannot have begun much before the year 1200, others doubted that such could have been the case. The texts we know are not free prose, transcribing a non-existent tape recording, but "book prose," which emerged from the hands of creative writers at the moment of writing. This was the perception that Hauch shared in forming.

Every introduction to the sagas of Icelanders – as well as many works that set themselves more ambitious goals – begins with an examination of the relative merits of "free prose" and "book prose."

Such a balancing will not be presented here. The last chapter will return briefly to the question, that is all. The purpose of what follows is not to give a first introduction to the large and remarkable literature that the sagas of Icelanders comprise, still less is the purpose to take up the debate of "free prose" versus "book prose" once again; the purpose is rather to explore some of the implications of the second theory, or perhaps more simply some of the implications of Carsten Hauch's lectures.

If we assume that Hauch was right in his belief that one can meaningfully seek out the "artistic design" in the sagas of Icelanders – and such an assumption is the basis of what follows – many paths lie open to the inquisitive reader. Some of these are discussed in the first part of the last chapter. Only one is followed in this book: that of taking the sagas seriously as works of art.

The general task of narratives based on history, asserted Hauch in the first of his lectures, is to show the hidden and inmost connections between events and in addition between these events and the human spirit (414). This is a Romantic manner of speaking but not necessarily mere rhetoric. In any case it can provide critical guidelines: what kinds of connection does the saga assert between the events – at times violent – that it relates, and between the events and the participants whose actions are their results or causes? What is the pattern that can be discerned in the individual saga or a series of sagas? These are the questions that have set the present work in motion.

It is not difficult to find the pattern formed by men preoccupied with honour and prestige, the power-hungry. Thus Hauch maintained that bloodfeud forms the "inmost center" of *Njal's Saga* (443) and that the imperative of bloodfeud and the code of honour is the driving force in most sagas of Icelanders. This interpretation has been repeated by many since.

Much less attention has been paid to the fact that beneath the pattern shaped by the drive for power a second pattern can be discerned which relates to sexual drives, drives which are generally thought to appear in the sagas of Icelanders only exceptionally. But clashes spurred on by sexual drives are not exceptional, rather they are the rule. And when things really go wrong in a saga it is usually because the two patterns have merged and work together. While the presence of one *or* the other is not enough to cross the threshold into action, the two combined set the catastrophe in motion. That things proceed in the manner just sketched is the thesis of this book. Much of it is given over to documenting this argument, the rest to reflecting on the reasons why the chaos caused by the combined forces of sex and power should be of such concern to the authors of sagas.

As we go along we shall gradually detect a myth nourished by the Icelanders concerning the rise and fall of their society. I shall also argue about the possible dates of composition of the sagas. Finally I shall have a word to say about what kind of historical situation gave rise to saga composition: what the challenge is to which saga composition may be seen to be a response.

I intend to spell out some implications of the "book prose" theory, the theory which says that the sagas came into existence when they were turned into books. But in actual fact the following analysis is independent of either theory in the debate that has so preoccupied saga scholarship. Strictly speaking, the only assumption required to read the sagas as I propose to do is that they mattered so much to the thirteenth century that many people spent considerable time and energy writing them, reading them, or hearing them read or recited. If the sagas received such a response in the thirteenth century – and there is every reason to believe that they did – then it would seem worthwhile to set them against that century, in order to enquire into the response, that is, to examine the vision they project and its relation to its time.

The nineteenth century taught us that a thing must be understood through its genesis. It was also the nineteenth century that determined the problems that saga scholarship should address. But like every landmark, the sagas of Icelanders can be viewed from many vantage points. The most visited vantage point is that centred on the "genesis" with all that it entails, i.e. interest in oral transmission, historical reliability, traditional material, literary reworking, author's personality. But the genetic view is not the only one. To choose another vantage point is not to deny the validity of what has been discovered, only to recognise that one cannot be in two places at the same time.

So this is not a balanced introduction to the sagas of Icelanders, but rather an attempt to establish a position from which to view the sagas of Icelanders. By adhering strictly to that point we may even hope to gain a more general insight into the act of reading.

I do not want to address myself to Old Icelandic specialists exclusively, because I know that the sagas of Icelanders occupy many beyond them, and because I believe that the problems that will emerge as we proceed concern many others. This has created a number of practical difficulties.

Of these my decision not to include a general introductory discussion concerning the sagas of Icelanders is the least; those who feel the lack of such a discussion can find it in some of the studies noted in the bibliography.

More difficult has been the problem of presenting the necessary documentation and of grafting my contribution on to the tree of scholarship without resorting to footnotes, which can all too easily function as a distraction and a makeshift. The solution that will be tried here consists of freeing the main exposition of references and then devoting a final chapter to such predecessors in saga scholarships as I need to take issue with or pay homage to.

The phrase "saga of Icelanders" is clumsy. In what follows it will often be replaced by the word "saga" alone, by which I will always intend "saga of Icelanders" unless it is prefixed by some qualifier. These particular sagas, often called the Icelandic family sagas, form one of the branches that tradition identifies within the whole of saga literature from the Icelandic Middle Ages; they are distinguished from *kings' sagas* in that their principal characters are uncrowned Icelanders, from *bishops' sagas* in that their characters are laymen, and from the *contemporary sagas* in that their events are set in a different period, from *sagas of olden times* partly in the time, partly also in the place in which their events take place, which for the better part of a saga of Icelanders is Iceland itself.

The division of the sagas into such categories is not original and ought perhaps to be ignored, as I shall argue. I respect the division, however, and stick to the single category that concerns me here for no other reason than expediency: to have a well-defined point of departure.

Quotations from the sagas are presented in English translation, for the trustworthiness of the analysis will gain little if it can be understood by only a few. The translated passages cited throughout are from the recently published five-volume collection *The Complete Sagas of Icelanders* (Reykjavik 1997). The editions of the Icelandic originals on which these translations are based are available in the *Íslenzk fornrit* series or the *Svart og hvitu* collections. The parenthesis immediately following each translated passage identifies its source, by chapter number and by volume and page in *The Complete Sagas of Icelanders*.

Since saga chapters are generally short and most editions and translations employ the same chapter divisions, the inclusion of chapter numbers will enable reference to alternative translations.

When secondary works are cited, they are identified in parenthesis by author's name and the date of publication, together with the page number. With this information it is possible to locate the source of the citation by referring to the bibliography where the more detailed information needed to address the work itself may be found.

Icelandic personal and place names are given in the form used in *The Complete Sagas of Icelanders,* which followed the policy of naturalizing names in English, rather than trying rigorously to reproduce the original. After initial citation I have preferred the more traditional names applied to individual sagas when the usage in *The Complete Sagas of Icelanders* seemed idiosyncratic or cumbersome: thus, for example, *Laxdœla Saga* rather than *The Saga of the People of Laxardal.*

Now to the sagas. In what does the interconnection between their events consist and between these and the human spirit? What does this interconnection have to teach us?

CHAPTER I

THE SECOND PATTERN

Thorolf's Saga

The sagas of Icelanders never begin *in medias res*. For the most part they anchor the story to be told in the historical reality to which it is supposed to belong, with the help of genealogies and frequently also with short narratives about the lives of the heroes' ancestors, their quarrels with Norwegian royal power, their journey to Iceland and their settling there.

Seldom, however, is the pre-history as long as it is in *Egil's Saga*, a third of whose 90 chapters have passed before the hero's name is first mentioned. One can regard this as putting the reader's patience to the proof, at least if the main thing is to get to the story about Egil. Whether indeed that *is* the main thing about the saga, as most discussions of *Egil's Saga* seem to have assumed, is a question to which we must return. What can be said is that the pre-history, at least when it is as long as it is in the case of *Egil's Saga*, appears on first reading to be a tale in its own right, an entire saga, the story of Thorolf, the central character's uncle: it has its own pre-history (c. 1-5) and it tells us (c. 6-21) about a man, his place in society, his conflict with other members – particularly *one* other member – of the society, about the conflict's escalation into murder (c. 22), the vengeance wreaked (c. 23), and finally (c. 24-27) about the reconciliation of the opponents.

"Thorolf's Saga" is a saga within a saga, more clearly shaped and marked by a greater sense of closure than the saga as a whole. We shall begin by trying to view it as a free-standing construction, in other words we will consider how it coheres, what it tells of, and why it proceeds as it does.

Thorolf is a magnificent man. At the beginning of the saga he is introduced in the following way:

> Thorolf was an attractive and highly accomplished man. He took after his mother's side of the family, a cheerful, generous man, energetic and very eager to prove his worth. He was popular with everyone. (c. 1, I 34)

The last phrase in particular is typical saga style: when the saga writer wants to render a straight-forward judgement, he prefers to withdraw behind the assessment of another. When he wants to pass a judgement about which there can be absolutely no doubt, that other person is called "everybody." Concerning the two men who commit the first assault on Thorolf, the narrator employs such a means to frame the judgement that they "were not popular among the common people" (c. 18, I 51).

This Thorolf suffers a violent death. By means of the worthiness ascribed to Thorolf, the saga lets the reader know that this is a lamentable occurrence and an evil one — the kind of evil that a lyric poem might lament. The saga itself is the opposite of lyrical: a study of the grounds of the evil, an interpretation of its roots. Reduced to its very minimum, the saga can be understood as an answer to the question: why do things go so badly for a good man? what is it in the order of existence that brings about this disorder?

It is no accident that it is the king who is Thorolf's slayer (c. 22). The most conspicuous conflict in the saga occurs between the king who is consolidating his power on the one side, and the free men on the other side who strive against or reluctantly give in to the new centralization.

Thorolf's father Kveldulf is numbered among the resisters. He has absolutely no desire to take on Harald Fair-hair (c. 3), but neither will he enter his service (c. 5). Passive resistance is his strategy, his evil presentiments his motive: "I think we will end up losing our lives because of that king" (c. 6, I 37). These misgivings recur as a kind of ground bass. It is hardly surprising that a conflict should arise between the king and Kveldulf's family.

But it is surprising that Thorolf of all people should be the one destroyed. For Thorolf is described as a man of the new order: opposed to his father and his father's judgement. In the conversation between the father and the son that takes place before Thorolf comes to his decision (c. 6), Thorolf explains his desire to join the king: the housecarls comprise only outstanding men; the king advances those who serve among them; and, besides, one can see that things go downhill for those who do not join the king. Thorolf's reasoning is practical and unproblematic. But in his father's warning one can see a possible hint of what will happen to him: "just avoid aiming too high or contending with stronger men than yourself" (c. 6). Perhaps Thorolf falls because he does not know his place.

The difficulty with raising this question, as well as a series of similar ones in what follows, is that one has to rely on the saga's values rather than on one's own. Our understanding of the saga is not improved by asking ourselves whether we consider Thorolf a great fellow or an arrogant social climber. Only when we have established what the saga writer thinks, are we entitled to the one value judgement that is the reader's prerogative: whether or not we approve the view of existence implied in the saga. Before we can accomplish this judgement, we have to understand the views and values propounded by the saga.

Whatever the question of Thorolf's relation to power and glory, he is truly placed in an ambiguous situation very soon after he attaches himself to the king. The king is on a summer trip and Thorolf decides to throw a fine party for him. He fits out a barn to this end and invites as many as five hundred men against the king's three hundred.

> The king sat in the high-seat, and when the upper and lower benches were both filled he looked around, very red in the face. He did not speak a word, but it seemed obvious he was angry. (c. 11, I 44)

What has happened is that the king has begun to suspect a threat. This was what an approaching ambush looked like. But there is nothing in the text to suggest that Thorolf had any sinister intentions. On the contrary, we have just been reminded of all Thorolf's many good traits at the end of the preceding chapter.

As events play out it becomes clear that he is by no means hopelessly naive. It dawns on him that the king might experience the sumptuous feast as a threat, a warning of rivalry and perhaps also of a planned burning-in. Thorolf, who is an outgoing, uncomplicated man, unlike his father and brother, tries to allay this suspicion by speaking straightforwardly, and in this way – and by means of a costly gift – he manages to clear things up.

Thorolf has been given a task by the king: to collect tax from the Lapps living in the mountains. This task he performs loyally, as the saga tells it. Then a coolness develops between the king and Thorolf, Harald rescinds his commission. Thorolf puts up with this. The next move on the king's part is a crime that he lets some of his men commit against one of Thorolf's men, the theft of a large, costly ship. Only now when the king is no longer content simply to take back what he himself has given, but launches a direct assault on Thorolf, who rightly feels blameless, Thorolf decides, as a man of honour, to take vengeance by inflicting the same injury on the king. The rest is just a matter of time. Thorolf has embarked on a struggle with his lord, the king, and there can be only one end to that.

What complicates our interpretation of the saga's value system is the difficulty in putting one's finger on Thorolf's "error." If he is to appear as a man of distinction and not a coward, he can hardly wait longer than he does to react to the injustice to which he has been subjected. If he had made plans to outmanoeuvre the king by means of guile, there ought to be signs of it in the text. And if the idea is to have him appear as merely naive, there would be no point in showing him to be capable of putting himself in the king's shoes and removing the misunderstandings that his actions had inadvertently occasioned.

Thorolf's most basic error is the very decision to enter the king's service. It was something he need not have done. Were "Thorolf's Saga" an isolated story, we might perhaps be unable to get beyond this judgement. We might have to settle for the possibility that this is the most cogent lesson to be learned from the saga: stay clear of kings. But "Thorolf's Saga" is actually part of a larger saga which contextualizes this possibility, as we shall later see. There are already signs, however, that this is neither the last nor the weightiest word that the saga has to say on the subject.

If we turn from Thorolf to King Harald, the man we meet is by no means a scoundrel. Harald, understandably enough, is a mistrustful lord, on the lookout for any changes in his domain. But he is aware of Thorolf's good qualities and he destroys him only reluctantly. His first comment on Thorolf (c. 8) is that he looks very "manly"; his next to last, before the murder, directed to two of his supporters: "Thorolf is more than a match for you, even though you consider yourselves men of strength and accomplishment"(c. 21, I 54). The plain fact is that a conflict would never have arisen between the two of them, if a third party had not come between them and orchestrated the whole wretched business.

This third party consists of the two sons of Hildirid. Without them the story of Thorolf's life and death would never have become a saga.

The two men have it in for Thorolf, but they are too weak and unimportant to carry out their project. What they lack in physical force to accomplish themselves, however, they make up in the cunning by which they get another to act for them.

This other person must be stronger than they are themselves and stronger than Thorolf. But he needs to be someone who is so placed as to feel threatened by Thorolf. These two requirements point to Harald Fair-hair: he is a king and he is afraid of anyone taking his measure.

Hildirid's sons understand precisely where they should drive in their wedge. It is a matter of transforming the king's secret anxiety into a real fear of Thorolf. The means is slanderous reports. But because of the relationship between the king and Thorolf, the required slanders must be numerous and crafty, if they are going to work. And they really are guileful.

The starting point that they choose is the best imaginable, for it is the one situation in which the king himself conceived a mistrust of Thorolf, the great feast at which Thorolf appeared with more supporters than his guest had.

Opportunity beckons later that same summer when the king goes to a feast at the home of the two malcontents. If at Thorolf's there had been too many, at the sons of Hildirid's feast "there were not many other people"(c. 12, I 44). Thorolf's many men are presented in the saga (at the end of Chapter 10) as an expression of this excellent man's popularity. When Harek and Hraerek – for these are their names – are shortly afterwards presented in exactly opposite circumstances, it should be read as an indication of their standing amongst the other members of their society. But their strength lies in their ability to reinterpret the past. Concerning Thorolf's feast they tell the king:

> . . . more was lavished on the feast than anywhere else too. But you were very fortunate that it turned out that you did not find your life in danger. Of course, someone as outstandingly wise and fortunate as you was likely to suspect a plot when you saw the great crowd that was gathered there. I'm told you had all your men fully armed or kept a safe watch both day and night. (c. 12, I 44)

They latch onto the king's own half-forgotten seed of a doubt. Not content simply to remind him of this – he might dismiss it, since he has already set it aside in view of Thorolf's behaviour – they present *proofs* that it actually existed: the king himself treated the feast as suspicious, they remind him. And with deft calculation they add to this the *flattering* references to his discernment.

On this basis they are able to reconstruct the whole course of events so that Thorolf's motives appear to the king in a way that suits their needs. Nor indeed do they spare the little trick that the greatest literary slanderer, Shakespeare's Iago, uses so brilliantly, namely breaking off at the decisive moment, which leaves the slanderer's victim begging to hear more. According to their account, events had proceeded as follows.

The common people are on the point of rising up (which is what the king must fear). All that is lacking is a leader (and the king knows that Thorolf has leadership capacities). In fact an army had assembled against the king with Thorolf as leader. It was larger than the king's following. Nevertheless they stopped the attack because "those farmers were terrified when they saw you come sailing up" (c. 12, I 45). Instead Thorolf chose burning-in. Evidence of this was his decision to hold the feast in a granary, so that he might avoid burning down his own house. The other evidence is that there were weapons on the walls.

The strategy by which they attain conviction is worth study. Only when, by various means, they have rendered probable the suggested course of events, does the real lying begin. And the weakest point – namely why the rebels did not follow up on their original plan and proceed with the attack on him when by singular good fortune they had the king, accompanied by only a small force, in their own territory – this point is camouflaged by the best device available to the slanderer: flattery. Less skilful people would have slid as quickly as possible over their weak point. Hildirid's sons know that flattery blinds its victims and convert this weakness into a strength – the king is so daunting that Thorolf and his folk were afraid!

The next information we get about Thorolf – that for the moment he happens not to be at home – they can easily assimilate to their established manner of devious interpretation: naturally he has made off for fear of being caught.

So sure are the two that their project will succeed that already in their first conversation they make no secret about their being available should the king think fit to confiscate Thorolf's feudal rights in Halagoland.

Nevertheless the first campaign produces no results. To be sure the king conceives deep and lasting suspicions. But since he has received the Lapp's tax that Thorolf had collected, from one of Thorolf's men, and since he can see with his own eyes that this tax has not been skimmed and the others among the housecarls speak against the suspicion, the king bides his time.

Thorolf does the same, although he hears the evil rumours. He is full of confidence, because he knows that he harbours no ambitions to become king.

So the sons of Hildirid must try again, which they proceed to do using as their starting point the tax that the king has received, the very thing that stilled his suspicions previously, because the tribute was "much more than ever before and much better quality of goods as well"(c. 13, I 46). But this does not prove that it *could* not have been yet larger and better. It is still possible that Thorolf has kept something for himself. All that Harek and Hraerek do on this second campaign is to show the king that the quantity of the tribute provides no grounds for letting his suspicions cool.

This time it works. The king withdraws his concessions and assigns them to the sons of Hildirid the next time Thorolf returns to him with the Lapp tax. This means demotion, but not destruction: he takes up his place among the housecarls again; he puts up with it.

The sons of Hildirid are not content with a half victory. They have it in for Thorolf. They turn out to be less successful in the collection of the Lapp tax than Thorolf was. The Lapps respect them less. The king reproaches them for the small yield, but they claim that Thorolf has taken the spoils right from under their noses. Conceal your own incompetence and malign your enemy: by such a strategy a clever slanderer can kill two birds with one stone.

So the king gives instructions that they should steal a ship from Thorolf in compensation for the valuables that he thinks himself to have been cheated of. They do so. Thorolf strikes a counter-blow. And then the game is up.

The sons of Hildirid are thus the axis on which the whole saga turns. Its two principal characters, Thorolf and the king, must fall out in one way or another for the deadly conflict to arise. It is here that the brothers enter as a third party seeking to *use* one against the other and therefore interested in setting misunderstandings loose. A study of how they go about their task shows how much they know about entering another person's consciousness to make it serve their ends. Which in turn shows how much the saga writer knows about such things.

What it does not explain is *why* they do it. In its exploration of causality the saga might have concluded with the melancholy fact that small men envy greater ones. But it does not. The sons of Hildirid have a bone to pick with Thorolf specifically, not with important and popular men in general. To be precise, he possesses the goods and the rights that they believe properly belong to them.

In the legalistic imagery of the saga, the situation is this: Thorolf's best friend and fellow housecarl is named Bard. It is from him that Thorolf has received his possessions (and his wife); that it should be so, was his friend's last wish before he fell in battle. The king and the family bless this bequest and the new marriage. Not until this moment do the sons of Hildirid have anything against Thorolf: it is the possessions they are after, which they think belong rightfully to them. They take on Thorolf not out of personal dislike, but because he withholds these possessions from them.

In this they believe themselves to be wholly justified, for these possessions come from a man, Bjorgolf, who was Bard's grandfather and their father. Bard, and before him his father, have on the other hand thought themselves equally justified in rejecting the claims of the sons of Hildirid.

With this we arrive at the story's earliest conflict. It is important for the evaluation of everything that follows to understand and evaluate this conflict correctly.

In the eyes of Bard and his father, the sons of Hildirid are the illegitimate offspring of Bjorgolf. The brothers reject this and believe that in every respect they have the right to be recognised as their father's sons. Their failure to carry this point is what sets the entire narrative in motion.

The story of violent erotic display, which comes late in the life of old Bjorgolf, may be summarized as follows.

Bjorgolf is a grandfather and a widower when, together with his son and grandson, he becomes infatuated with a young girl, Hildirid, with whom he is paired off during the drinking one evening at an autumn feast.

When old wood catches fire, it flares up quickly. Bjorgolf cannot wait to possess himself of Hildirid. Right after the feast he, together with a large armed escort, goes off to Hildirid's father, intending to have his way with the girl:

> "The reason I have come here is to take your daughter home with me and I shall celebrate our wedding here now."
> Hogni saw he had no other choice than to let Bjorgolf have his way. (c. 7, I 39)

The Old Icelandic word here translated as "wedding" is *lausabrullaup*, a word whose exact meaning is disputed. But to cut through the legal debate that has surrounded the issue – see Bley (1909) and the Íslenzk fornrit notes – Bjorgolf has his way by force, against the wishes of the family; of this there can be no doubt. In this respect, in any event, his behaviour is "unlawful."

The legitimate son denounces the result of this unlawful erotic act: the sons of Hildirid. The same is true of the next inheritor, the grandson Bard.

The description of this asocial wedding is in every respect a contrast to Bard's marriage, which comprises a network of agreements and family approvals. The notion of "agreement" – rendered by a variety of synonyms: *heitit, bundit, halda, ákvedit* – dominates the description. The orderliness is repeated when this girl, now a widow, is married a second time – to Thorolf. The wishes of the dead man, of her father and of the king are uppermost. Marriage is a social arrangement. So the social dimension, as opposed to the erotic, is what dominates the saga's description of these marriages.

But this does not mean that the erotic is not a powerful impulse among these people, quite the contrary. When one excavates its deepest roots "Thorolf's Saga" is a story – if ever there was one – about the havoc the erotic urge can cause when it is *not*, as in the cases of Bard and Thorolf, confined within acceptable social channels, but flows freely wherever the impulse takes it.

Bjorgolf's spontaneous act is a breaking of the order that holds society together. Bjorgolf is described as "descended from a mountain giant" (c. 7, I 38), which makes his role as the breaker of rules clearer. And once the rules are broken, the consequences roll through the generations, laying waste indiscriminately. The sons of Hildirid react most reasonably against an exclusion that is none of their doing. Thorolf inherits from his friend Bard a property that he had not built up, but on the same occasion he inherits some liabilities that he has also done nothing to incur. Thus a good man is brought down.

By way of summary, the power relationships around the king and between the king and his powerful followers are the initial cause of the course of Thorolf's story. Had such a pattern, which is sustained by the urge to power, not existed, the sons of Hildirid would not have found an arena in which to exercise their skills.

But the constellation of Thorolf/King Harald, which is the most conspicuous feature of the tale, is not in itself enough to explain the course of events. If we looked no further, we would conclude that the saga's message is to steer clear of kings, as Kveldulf says. End of story.

When we observe the catalysts of the catastrophe, the sons of Hildirid, we add a further ingredient – the not very interesting truth that great men are envied by small. But if we go a little further into the backwards revelation of the saga and ask why the sons of Hildirid have come to the position that they have, we find an answer in the text, and the answer makes it clear that it is not a case of any particular jealousy that they feel towards Thorolf. By and large the assumptions of individual psychology do not have very much to do with the course of events. But at the heart of the brothers' existence, of society's repression of them, and thereby of the threat that they pose to society, lies a manifestation of the *erotic drive* at an abnormal moment, in an abnormal mode, which is contrasted to the well-regulated, socially-approved playing out of the same drive in ideal men like Bard and Thorolf.

The saga's first pattern involves the urge to power. The saga's second pattern testifies to the erotic drive as a dangerous force that breaks down order and causes events to unfold blindly. It would be quite correct to call the saga a love story, if by "love story" we mean not the sweet and tender stuff of romantic love, but a story of how dangerous the power of love is, once it is allowed to develop unchecked.

At this time elsewhere in Europe medieval troubadours were singing about the pleasures of feeling a love forbidden by the rules of society. The saga writer tells of how dangerous it is to follow the impulse that goes with such emotions.

Or rather the writer of "Thorolf's Saga" does: that is all we have established thus far. The next task is to investigate whether this analysis of the structure of Thorolf's story casts any light on *Egil's Saga*, to which it is indeed only the prelude.

Egil Skallagrimsson's Saga

The story of Egil is saturated with power struggles, violent acts, and obstinacy. It is full of head-on collisions between great men standing on their rights.

The first story related of Egil (c. 40) tells how he, as a boy of less than twelve, slew a playmate because of a disagreement about a game. And one of the last stories about the aged Egil (c. 83 ff) shows how, in a struggle between his sons and those of a friend, which was about to end in a settlement, he uses his power to have it his own way regardless. One of the characteristics that distinguishes sagas from the novels of the last two hundred years is that they are not stories of personal development, at least not in the Romantic or Naturalistic meaning of the phrase. The traits that determine behaviour are in operation from first to last, in the child as well as in the aged man.

Egil's life is a struggle for freedom of action, a struggle against the forces that seek to limit his freedom. The most obvious of these forces is the urge to power that drives other men. The first pattern of the saga emerges in the collision between such urges.

The collision is anticipated in every detail in the story of childhood play. Egil has drawn by lot as his opponent a ten or eleven year old boy named Grim – the game is a competition, one against one. Egil cannot cope with this Grim, which does not mean that Grim holds back in the struggle. So Egil uses his bat on Grim, but gains nothing except to be knocked to the ground himself and ignominiously beaten. Egil, who began the escalation, has now exhausted all the physical resources he possesses, but not thereby his desire for vengeance. The next possibility is to find allies. So Egil quits the game, goes to visit Thord, gets an axe from him and slays his opponent with it.

Here we have Egil in a nutshell. He wants elbow room. When he is prevented from getting it, he uses physical force, and when that does not suffice, skill and cunning. Later he also uses a sense of justice, but only a sense of the justice owed to him which cannot therefore be distinguished from his drive for power.

Egil is well content with the outcome of the game and so are his companions. The saga-writer evidently shares their satisfaction: Egil himself composes his first verse, his mother talks of the viking in him, certainly he must get himself a ship; the narrative is so constructed that readers feel no sympathy for the slain playmate and that they focus their attention purely and simply on the viking to be. Immediately afterwards we see how Skallagrim, Egil's father, who is already known as a man of rank, behaves in the same way as Egil.

This scene acquaints us with Egil the powerful. Later on his projects become bigger, his opponents stronger, and his strategies more subtle. But in all essentials they are the same as we have seen in the childhood game.

His opponents in the struggle for influence become by turns a series of different men in various lands – Courland, England, Varmland – and King Erik Bloodaxe in his ancestral country, Norway. Against the former the struggle is always more or less a fight about who is the stronger and who will therefore control the other and his goods. Egil wins these contests without exception.

Against King Erik the struggle is more complicated. There can be no doubt that the drive for power is one of its motives. But on the other hand it would be incorrect to imagine that Egil is striving to become King of Norway. This is even less likely than that his uncle Thorolf should have wanted the throne. Thorolf strove for a position of great influence. Egil steers clear of administrative authority, but on the other hand gathers absolutely no allies in his struggle against it.

If we consider *Egil's Saga* simply as the story of a collision between two men with an urge to power, or perhaps as a collision between two forms of power, the old fashioned free-man and the power of a modern monarchy, it is difficult to avoid the conclusion – drawn by more than one reader – that it is an incoherent and unnecessarily convoluted story, exciting at times, and perhaps indeed historically interesting, but complicated and long-winded.

Much of the saga can, it is true, be explained in terms of men's drive for power. But behind everything lies a long series of incidents which first form a coherent picture when we assume that humankind is subject to another conflictual drive, the erotic.

This assumption has not as a rule informed readings of *Egil's Saga*. It therefore demands a thorough-going demonstration. That the following discussion will be more detailed than the foregoing one should not lead anyone to the conclusion that the sexual drive is the one and only explanatory force. It is not. Without the drive for power, no saga. But with nothing but the drive for power, no adequate reading of the saga.

The suspicion that something is missing may arise when one examines the relationship between Egil and King Erik. It appears, to be precise, that Erik must be somewhat forgetful of this relationship, since he needs to be reminded constantly that Egil is his enemy. You will probably allow yourself to be persuaded to forget what harm he has done to you, King Erik is told (c. 48) at the beginning of their long antagonism; have him taken out at once and beheaded is the advice to Erik many years later (c. 60), nevertheless the king lets Egil live on in unchanged circumstances. It does not seem as if Erik burns with enmity towards Egil, whereas the speaker certainly does, and she is the same in both episodes – and several similar ones – Queen Gunnhild.

King Erik does not do anything to Egil that Gunnhild cannot be seen to have instigated. The strife between Egil and royal authority arises at the moment that he and Gunnhild meet, and it endures as long as she appears in the saga. So there are good grounds for a closer examination of the relationship between the two and what the saga says about it.

Gunnhild is first named in Chapter 37. It is said of her there that she was "outstandingly attractive and wise, and well versed in the magic arts" and that Thorolf – the nephew of the first Thorolf and brother of Egil – and Gunnhild "struck up a close friendship" (c. 37, I 75). Already the description of her – as beautiful and skilled in sorcery – points in a definite direction. Such a woman may represent danger for a man.

The second time she is spoken of, the first time she actually enters the saga, is when she and Egil meet face to face at the feast where they conceive a lifelong hatred for one another (c. 44). The scene demands a closer examination, which will follow. Afterwards we see her, as already mentioned, inciting Erik against Egil (c. 48, c. 57, c. 60); we see her inciting her brother against Egil (c. 49); we hear Egil being warned against her by his friend Arinbjorn (c. 56); we hear that she is colluding with Egil's enemy Berg-Onund in the great struggle over inheritance that makes up the middle part of the saga (c. 57); we encounter Egil's verse about her, which describes her as the great opponent and bird of ill omen in his life (c. 58); we see Egil kill her son Rognvald, a death which has appeared to other interpreters (for example, Andersson 1967, 107) as meaningless (c. 58); we observe Egil setting up the "scorn-pole" against her and her husband (c. 58); we see her attempt to prevent Egil from redeeming his head, when he falls into the hands of the Norwegian king and queen in York (c. 60); and we hear finally that she as an old widow settles in Denmark and that Egil is advised by his friend Arinbjorn to avoid Denmark (c. 48). He follows the advice. The worst he afterwards suffers comes from another corner: old age and death, the loss of his son.

The connection with Gunnhild, or rather the hostile *dis*connection between them, runs like a thread through all of Egil's struggles with royal authority and his greatest and most protracted inheritance struggle. We shall see how that begins.

But to prepare the ground, it is necessary to look at the other relationship that plays a vital role in Egil's life, that with Asgerd, his wife.

He marries her late after some resistance on her part. When she becomes a widow Egil visits her and offers her his support. She receives the offer "fittingly, but played the matter down" (c. 56, I 102). Egil's action requires no further elucidation than that he is the brother of her dead husband. But his response to her reticence shows that he was not just fulfilling his familial duties.

> As autumn progressed Egil grew melancholy and would often sit down with his head bowed into his cloak. (c. 56, I 102)

His friend Arinbjorn thinks that Egil must be grieving for his brother's death. But then Egil recites one of his obscure poems. And at his friend's query he interprets the poem:

> "I shall answer your question who the woman is that I make poems about. It is your kinswoman Asgerd, and I would like your support in arranging this marriage." (c. 56, I 103)

He gets the help he seeks. Asgerd, however, is just as passive when he proposes as she was before. She refers him to the family; in response to Arinbjorn's inquiry she does the same thing. The family is in favour, hence a marriage is the result.

The narrator has made it quite clear that Egil has encountered a human relationship in which he must confront his own shortcomings and where power is no help. Egil's love is great and unrequited. A love so strong that its symptoms can very nearly be mistaken for sorrow over a brother's death does not spring up overnight. There were in fact signs of it earlier in the saga.

When Egil's brother Thorolf as a young man wants to leave on his second trip abroad and wishes to take along Asgerd, who has been fostered by the brothers' father at Borg, Egil's determination that he be brought along makes him so unruly that Thorolf is forced to take him (c. 39-41). As it later turns out, Thorolf's purpose in having Asgerd travel with him to her family in Norway is to propose to her.

Egil's insistence does not seem to beg an explanation. It could be nothing more than the desire to travel abroad that drives him; that would fit very well with the Egil we have come to know at that point.

More striking, on the other hand, is Egil's becoming unwell on the very day that Thorolf sets out for his wedding, "Egil fell ill and was unable to join him" (c. 42, I 80). But the moment the wedding party has left for the feast he becomes so energetic that he must himself be on his way. In the understated rhetoric of the saga, this is a relatively clear indication that the wedding which is taking place is not a matter of indifference to Egil.

When the saga at last talks directly of Egil's love for Asgerd, it turns out to be a love of enormous dimensions, like everything else about this man. It is not especially odd that there are traces of it earlier in the narrative, nor odd – given the saga's style – that these hints are hidden.

The meeting between Egil and Gunnhild takes place just when Egil, who had suddenly become "sick," has with equal suddenness become quite well again, which should not be passed over as an accidental detail. Egil is in an excited state when he meets the woman that the saga has introduced as beautiful and skilled in magic and who at the time of the saga's composition was surely known elsewhere as a cruelly erotic woman; see for example the story told in *The Saga of Harald Fairhair* (Chapter 33 in *Heimskringla*) of Erik Bloodaxe's finding her in the arms of two Lapps who are equally enamoured and skilled in magic.

Egil and the Olvir he is travelling with arrive at a farm on Atloy run by a certain Bard, where they are entertained modestly in a little house on the property, while a royal reception is taking place in the main building. The king notes at a particular moment that his steward is gone and asks whether Bard's other guests, whom he is apparently off looking after, may not be invited in (c. 44).

The king bids Olvir sit opposite him, and Egil, as the text points out, sits beside Olvir. It is not recorded who it was that he comes to sit opposite. It might be supposed that the queen sat elsewhere in the hall, on a cross-bench together with the other women, which seems the commonest practice in the sagas, as for example in Chapter 71 of this saga where the women of the household sit together in this way. But it is certainly not impossible, considering the importance of the queen, that she sits at the side of her husband, in which case she faces Egil. It would be like the saga to provide such information in this indirect way. Whatever we are to make of this detail, a tense relationship develops between these two, a relationship which endures throughout most of the saga.

Egil drinks like one possessed and abuses the steward – in verse – for keeping the good liquor for the fancy guests within. The steward contrives with the queen to put poison in his ale, but Egil protects himself against its effect by means of magic. In the end Egil leaves the party and kills the steward.

It would not be overstating the case to say that this behaviour witnesses to a man in a state of intense inner turmoil. At the moment when his apparently long-cherished hopes that he will some day gain Asgerd are definitively dashed by his brother's marriage to her, he meets a woman who is an emblem of the erotic according to this and other sagas, but who yet remains a still less possible object of his erotic urges than does Asgerd. All the conditions for a love-hate relationship are in place.

One can choose to understand the magic as a curious, folkloristic museum piece and nothing else, but then the scene is merely incomprehensible. One can also choose to understand it as an expression of the powers of eroticism, in which case the scene falls into place as the source of the long-enduring attraction and repulsion between Egil and Gunnhild, which causes so much discord in the rest of the saga.

The use of magic in other places in the narrative supports this interpretation.

Certainly it is the king who responds in the first place. He can hardly do otherwise, when his steward has been killed. But that the killing in itself is not enough to set in motion the protracted conflict is shown by Gunnhild's repeated need to stiffen his resolve afterwards. Neither of the two parties in the struggle express themselves clearly on this subject. Egil almost never refers to Gunnhild separately from the king. And Gunnhild speaks of the Skallagrimssons when she is trying to egg her brothers on (c. 49). But we know from before (c. 37) that Thorolf enjoyed her favour and that he never did anything to spoil their relationship; so we can draw our own conclusions. Gunnhild and Egil are the primary adversaries in the conflict. Its ramifications must be traced to the hostility between them.

The saga is constructed in such a way – as we have already seen in the Asgerd-narrative – that the premises of a scene are first presented long after the scene. Reading sagas requires a good memory. An important premise in the understanding of Egil's erotic sufferings emerges only late in the saga: Egil is ugly.

> Egil had very distinctive features, with a wide forehead, bushy brows and a nose that was not long but extremely broad. His beard grew over a long, broad part of his face, and his chin and entire jaw were exceptionally broad. With his thick neck and broad shoulders, he stood out from other men. When he was angry, his face grew harsh and fierce. He was well built and taller than other men, with thick wolf-grey hair, although he had gone bald at an early age. (c. 55, I 100)

This is not what the sagas consider a handsome appearance. Nor is it – and this is just as important – what Egil himself considers handsome, as we see in his own words when he ransoms his head, which is to say his life, from King Erik in York (c. 62). It stands to reason that such a man has difficulty satisfying his sexual urges. This is where this potent man meets insurmountable obstacles. The consequences of his shortcomings are fierce conflicts and great damage.

The theme is played out in miniature when Egil visits Earl Arnfinn (c. 48). A so-called *tvímenning* is supposed to take place in the evening; that is, men and women are going to drink together, two by two; just as when old Bjorgolf became infatuated with Hildirid. By means of the drawing of lots he wins the beautiful daughter of the earl, but she will have nothing to do with him until he has indirectly showed himself to be a courteous man – through a poem. Egil is anything but a lady's man, which is the source of one of the most insurmountable obstacles he struggles against.

This expresses itself at greatest length in the inheritance struggle with Berg-Onund and most dramatically with the head-ransoming in York. The former story goes like this.

There is some doubt as to the inheritance rights of Asgerd, Egil's wife, as a result of her being the fruit of a "wild" relationship. Her father, Bjorn the Landowner, took her mother, Thora, with Thora's consent, but without that of her family. Once again an ungovernable erotic urge has sowed the seeds of conflict, as in "Thorolf's Saga." Egil insists on his wife's rights, and Berg-Onund who is married to Asgerd's half sister asserts his own. When Egil decides to pursue the matter seriously, he discovers that Queen Gunnhild supports Berg-Onund. The new inheritance struggle thus becomes available for use as an ingredient in the old struggle between Egil and the royal couple (c. 56).

The first round of this contest concludes when King Erik, strongly urged by Gunnhild, who now tells her husband that surely Egil aspires to his royal power, declares Egil banished from Norway. When Egil gets to Iceland he manages to have his opponent Berg-Onund murdered, and Erik and Gunnhild's ten-year-old son into the bargain, and he sets up a scorn-pole against the parents of the murdered boy (c. 58). The second round (c. 66) ends when Egil gets the property to which he believes he has a claim.

In between occurs the most dangerous event in his life, the trip to York and his last meeting with Gunnhild.

Things have gone downhill for the royal pair. King Hakon, foster-son to King Athelstan, has driven his brother from the throne in Norway. Erik has taken flight and after a struggle has concluded a treaty with King Athelstan in England, whose vassal he has become. He has fought on his behalf in the battle that cost his brother his life. In this indirect way the saga indicates that a change has taken place in the power relationship between Egil and the Norwegian royal couple.

Before Egil's journey the following remark occurs:

> It is said that Gunnhild had a magic rite performed to curse Egil Skalla-grimsson from ever finding peace in Iceland until she had seen him. (c. 60, I 116)

Once again magic acts in a manner which is perfectly understandable, if one sees it as an expression of erotic forces. One does not need to suppose that any telepathy is involved to understand Egil's unrest; he has borne the seeds of unrest within him for a long time.

So he goes to England, suffers shipwreck and falls into the hands of his mortal enemy. She does what she can to get her husband to kill him on the spot. But Arinbjorn's persuasion and the king's reasonableness give Egil a chance: he is granted a night to compose his false encomium to Erik, the "Head-Ransom." After he has recited it, his life is spared by the impressed king; from this point on Gunnhild is not heard to speak; she has lost. Shortly afterwards Egil recovers his wife's inheritance in Norway.

If one asks what the poem means for Egil, the answer is this: life and death, quite simply and literally. In a very palpable sense his poetic ability saves Egil from death during his freely-chosen/enforced stay in York. To compose a skaldic poem means to satisfy some complicated and highly artificial rules; it is a performance. Egil composes equally well when the act of composing responds to the existential moment, as in "Sonatorrek," or when he composes under duress as in the encomium to King Erik in York.

Egil is first and foremost a performer. His strengths – physical and intellectual – are greater than those of other people and he is most alive when he is employing them.

There are no bounds to the physical strength he exhibits as a warrior in Courland (c. 46) and England (c. 52-55) and Frisland (c. 70). The saga makes use of a lofty, stylized mode in its warrior descriptions. As far as his intellectual development is concerned, the "Head-Ransom" is the yardstick: the poem serves to ransom his life when all other avenues are closed to him.

What limits him is the presence of another man who possesses greater power than he does, the king. The conflict that arises between them sets up the first conspicuous pattern in the saga. But a limitation of another kind is seen in a peculiar feature of Egil's erotic relations, namely that they are never straightforward or fortunate, but as regards the two crucial women in his life, either reluctant (Asgerd) or perverted (Gunnhild).

Young Egil's troubled relationship with Asgerd prepares for the mature man's ill-omened relationship with Gunnhild: Asgerd is finally lost to him on the day he collides with the satanic female on Norway's throne. And wretched relations between him and Gunnhild lead to the murders of Bard, the king's steward, and Thorvald, Egil's man; to the long, harrowing struggle for the inheritance that Gunnhild guards and to which Egil thinks himself entitled; to the murders of Berg-Onund and the unlucky Rognvald, Gunnhild's son. Power-hunger and erotic impulse are woven together in the saga's train of events, and neither of these urges can be dispensed with, if we are to understand Egil's turbulent existence. The story would be impossible if Erik with his royal power did not stand at Gunnhild's side. But it would be cut in half if Gunnhild, with her unquenchable thirst for the destruction of Egil, did not stand at Erik's side.

The conclusion of the saga after this turning point involves a few minor elaborations of motifs already stated.

A berserk by the name of Ljot has conceived an uncontrollable love for a beautiful young girl, a niece of Egil's friend Arinbjorn. She and her family refuse Ljot, who in response tries to accomplish his desire by challenging her brother to a duel. Egil intervenes and restores order by taking up the challenge on behalf of the brother and killing the berserk (c. 65).

On a voyage to Varmland that Egil has undertaken as a substitute for Arinbjorn – it is a dangerous trip and the new king probably intends to endanger the lives of his mortal enemies by setting them such a risky undertaking – Egil arrives at a house where Helga, the daughter of the family, lies sick. The illness has been caused by a young man from nearby who has carved runes against her. Egil avails himself of the same device and she begins to recover (c. 73).

Several chapters later the matter is addressed more directly:

> The man who had carved runes for Helga lived close by. It transpired that he had asked for her hand in marriage, but Thorfinn had refused him. Then the farmer's son had tried to seduce her, but she did not want him. After that he pretended to carve love runes to her, but did not know how to, and what he carved had caused her sickness instead. (c. 77, I 147)

Nowhere is the interconnection between the erotic and the magical more clearly expressed. It seems evident that we should treat this incident as a key, which in this case – as so often in the sagas – should be used to unlock the meaning of a foregoing action.

Egil's role in these two erotic episodes late in the saga is as a substitute, a helper. His own conflicts have played themselves out. The problems that remain to him are the matters of time and death, the two ultimate limitations on the freedom of movement he has won for himself.

He loses two sons and is on the point of committing suicide out of sorrow at the desolation he has to look forward to. But his daughter Thorgerd, who has inherited her father's cunning, arranges tempting food for him, awakening his will to live. So his life force once again can issue in a remarkable performance, the poem "Sonatorrek" (c. 79).

He involves himself in the strife between his surviving son and his neighbour's, once more displaying his endlessly assertive nature. Finally he arrives at dissolution as a doddering elder. Time has caught up with him and set his final limit.

Given all the foregoing, the two hitherto separated parts of *Egil's Saga* seem to merge and form an integrated whole. What has been called the second pattern runs through the whole text and unites it.

The forces that destroy order in the society and create conflicts – bloody and destructive conflicts – are not only people's drive for power, but also people's erotic urges.

We have seen that each of the three parties in "Thorolf's Saga" – Thorolf, Harald Fairhair and the sons of Hildirid – behaved rationally according to their lights. It is a mistake to maintain that the unhappy outcome is the king's fault – as F. Paasche asserted (1924) – and it is equally mistaken to maintain that the envy of Hildirid's sons should bear the blame – as P. Hallberg argued (1956). Similarly Thorolf could not really have behaved any differently than he did. The origins of the conflict can be traced back to an original "wild" action, an impulse which the rules and laws of society failed to channel, and whose fruit – two individuals at the margins of society – creates a basis for a conflict which by winding paths becomes a menace to orderly societal life causing death and destruction to innocent people.

The saga is saturated with such relationships which contrast with the orderly connections sanctioned by society. In the second chapter there is already talk of Olvir Hump who falls so unhappily in love that he can no longer fulfil his obligations as a man and go on a viking expedition, but gives himself over vainly to the writing of love poetry.

Bjorgolf and Hildirid are the first example of a wild relationship of narrative importance that develops in such a way that the man gains the woman by force. The results of this have been sufficiently discussed.

Bjorn Brynjolfsson and Thora follow their passions in fleeing from family and concealing from their family's friends how they behaved. The consequence of this becomes a source of contention concerning inheritance which is used in the saga's central narrative, the relationship between Gunnhild and Egil.

And finally, the last two stories, about Ljot and about Helga, reveal two further ways in which wildness can express itself: in duels and in rune carving.

The common element in all these "wild" relationships is that they entail risks to life and limb not only for the parties involved, but for other, often entirely blameless members of society. Love – this is the philosophy that emerges from the narrative – does not just concern the two persons involved; rather it is of societal concern and, when its energies are not channeled within the boundaries established by society, it is itself a menace to its very order.

Egil is a man who is larger than life when it comes to feats of power, whether in battle or in poetry. But he is like other men in that domain of life where his abilities are limited. He instigates conflicts so violent and dangerous that he must struggle to the utmost, both physically and intellectually, to survive them. The violent attraction-repulsion relationship between him and Gunnhild is the axis around which most of the story turns and which the remainder of the story plays out against, as either anticipation or reflection.

Human beings are driven by the urge for power, but also by the erotic urge. Both can be dangerous to society the moment that their expression disregards its rules.

If this conclusion does not sound terribly surprising, it is necessary to remind ourselves how sagas such as this one have normally been read. As Finnur Jónsson put it, in his *Litteraturhistorie* (I, 489): "In this way it becomes completely natural and understandable that Egil was not some sort of erotic character; and it is hard to tell whether he marries

Asgerd because he is attracted to her, or because he does not want her possessions and Thorolf's to fall into alien hands." Johannes V. Jensen, the Danish Nobel laureate, expresses himself similarly.

> One seeks in vain here only for the erotic sweetmeats familiar from the cinema. The saga contains no detailed picture of Egil's family life, such as we have of Napoleon's. When Egil's wife Asgerd died, he gave up his household and moved in with relatives at Mosfell – that is all the saga tells us. (*De isl. Sagaer* I, 18f)

Erotic sweetmeats? No, certainly not. Jensen manages indeed to set up his proposition in such a way that one has no choice but to accept it, if one has to swallow his value judgements as well.

But the thought behind the proposition is nevertheless skewed. The final sentence – "that is all the saga tells us" – indicates a reading that focuses entirely on the tall story or the tale of robbers, which is how Jensen refers to the saga in the same passage.

But the saga goes beyond the boy's adventure story. It does not deal only in gang-warfare or strong heroes. It understands impulses that the boy's adventure story knows nothing of. And it seems to demonstrate that these impulses are not a source of pleasure but a hazard to ordered life.

Laxdœla Saga

Laxdœla Saga is the same length as *Egil's Saga*, but broader in scope and more complex. It contains as many people as the telephone book of a middle-sized modern suburb – 350-400 are mentioned by name; it stretches from the time of settlement a good way into the Christian Middle Ages; it is not assembled around a single character like *Egil's Saga*, but around groups and generations, the inhabitants of Laxardal over the centuries. It is the people of the valley who constitute at once its subject matter and its problematic. Its hosts of incidents and characters together sketch the picture of a society troubled by internal difficulties that sometimes are overcome, sometimes come to a head in destructive conflicts. And like *Egil's Saga* it addresses the question of *why* things happen as they do.

Two narratives emerge from the welter of episodes, each dominating its half of the saga. In the first part it is the story of Olaf Peacock, the illegitimate son of a slave woman of royal descent, who gains a position of pre-eminence in Icelandic society by virtue of his possessions and his distinction. In the second part it is the story of Gudrun and Kjartan, who love one another, and Bolli, who marries Gudrun, and the ensuing conflict between the sworn brothers Kjartan and Bolli, which comes to a head in murder and revenge.

They would not seem to have much to do with each other: on the one hand, the tale of the disguised prince, whose lowly circumstances reveal themselves to have concealed a royal lineage, and whose course of life leads to his outer circumstances coming to match his descent and, on the other hand, the tale of the psychological love-triangle that proceeds in the way of heroic poetry to a tragic conclusion. The stories are harmonised stylistically by setting the princely fairy-tale in a realistic milieu and depicting the love story as the cause of havoc in the real life surrounding the three protagonists. Doubtless one could undertake a motif-analysis of the saga that would disassemble it and show the different literary origins of the two principle narratives, if one wanted to go hunting for them.

But one can also turn one's attention elsewhere. Seeing that the stories happen to be linked, one can ask what it is that unifies the total narrative. It may be the case that many literary sources are laid under contribution. However, this is scarcely done to delight readers or listeners with the message that the saga-writer was acquainted with such a variety of sources. Rather it may be done in order *to make use* of them to achieve something, to please readers and listeners with a good story doubtless, but surely at the same time to draw their attention to some truths. This proposition is in any event worth testing. To find these truths, if indeed there are such truths, requires that one begin by turning one's attention to what it is that binds the stories together.

The external binding element is kinship. The narrative focuses on three generations of the same family. And the core in each of these generations comprises two half-brothers or sworn-brothers. All three pairs come into conflict with each other and thereby threaten the social order precisely where a society such as that in the Icelandic free state period at once defines itself and is most vulnerable: the family. The sequence of events that make up the three different conflicts – the similarities, differences and links between them – constitute the heart of the statement that the saga makes.

The three pairs are Hoskuld and his half-brother Hrut; Hoskuld's sons, the half-brothers Thorleik and Olaf; and the sons of these two, who grow up as sworn-brothers in Olaf's household, Kjartan and Bolli. The first pair struggles, the second pair achieves reconciliation, and one member of the third pair kills the other. Together their stories create a picture whose outlines we shall trace.

A Conflict Arises
Setting aside for the moment the first person who emerges from the crowd of saga characters as a significant player, the second such person is Hoskuld. His father dies early and his mother who "was still a young and good-looking woman" (c. 7, V 7)) at the time, leaves for Norway, where she marries for a second time in compliance with *all* conventions and in this new marriage bears a son, Hrut. Her second husband dies of an illness, and she moves back to Iceland, leaving Hrut behind with his family in Norway but bearing her fortune, and settles down with her Icelandic son where she remains until her death,

> And Hoskuld took over all her wealth, although his brother Hrut was entitled to half. (c. 8, V 7)

Here lies the seed of a conflict that will later come to fruition. The saga writer has taken pains to establish that no illegality in the preceding generation underwrites this action. Hoskuld's mother has followed all the rules when she married a second time. It is Hoskuld who commits the first injustice when he takes possession of what is not his. Although he does what he can to maintain possession, nothing really drastic happens between him and his half-brother, since Hrut is a patient man who goes to great lengths to proceed justly:

> Hrut lived at Kambsnes for three years and sought continually to press Hoskuld for his property at assemblies and other legal gatherings, where he put his case well. Most men said that Hrut was in the right. (c. 19, V 22)

Only after this does Hrut move to a rather modest form of self-help. When Hoskuld wants to retaliate by killing his brother, his wise wife prevents the realization of his plan and the story ends at her instigation with an honourable settlement. But according to the saga, the honour belongs more to the woman and to Hrut than to Hoskuld.

What is said in plain language about Hoskuld is commendatory – this in a saga which is exceptionally given to evaluative language. Yet what is said of the two brothers' respective relationship to the law and justice indicates that they are not evaluated equally. Hoskuld never argues for the justice of what he has done, he seeks merely to maintain his position by force; Hrut seeks to obtain his rights from him by lawful means. And there are further indications that the brothers are evaluated differently.

One of these is that Hoskuld begets a son on his concubine and thus engenders the seeds of conflict in the next generation. The process by which this takes place differs, however, from the engendering of the similar conflict that we observed in *Egil's Saga*.

Early one summer Hoskuld goes to a place in Norway where a thing and a market are held. During the event men drink and chat, and Hoskuld not surprisingly finds himself in such a mood that he experiences the desire – as the saga puts it – "to purchase a slave woman" (c. 12, V 10).

A consultation takes place and, in a carefully described transaction between him and a merchant, Hoskuld becomes the owner of a mute slave woman. "Hoskuld then went back to his own booth. Hoskuld slept with the woman that same evening" (c. 12. V 11). This is the same mute woman who some years later, when she begins to talk, reveals herself to be Melkorka, daughter of an Irish king, taken into captivity and made a slave by Norwegian vikings on a raid; and it is this relationships that produces Olaf Peacock, the principal character in the next generation in Laxardal.

At first the situation causes some unrest in Hoskuld's home, as might be expected. The saga treats concubinage as a social reality, but this does not imply that women relished it, or that it did not provide occasions for problems.

Melkorka gives birth to a boy in Iceland, who at once shows himself to be special. Hoskuld's wife demands of her husband that the concubine be sent away or at least be required to work. Hoskuld chooses the latter and of all jobs sets her the task of serving the mistress of the farm. He shows similar psychological perspicacity when he at last hears the concubine speak and gets her to explain that she is actually a princess. His first reaction is to dash in to his wife with the news in order that she may share in his delight.

> Jorunn said there was no way of knowing whether she spoke the truth, and that she had no use for people of dubious origin. (c. 13, V 13)

After this it does not take long before the two women quite simply come to blows. Jorunn flings her stockings at Melkorka's head, who responds by giving her a bloody nose.

When two such women each have a son by the same man, the groundwork is laid for strife in the next generation. Of this Hoskuld is the unreflecting author.

In yet a third way, the saga-writer exhibits his unease with Hoskuld. The next narrative that contributes to the delineation of Hoskuld's character is a hugely complicated episode involving two hitherto unmentioned brothers who come to blows over a trifle (c. 14-16). When this complicated sideshow has played itself out and the story returns to the main action, it happens that Hoskuld is associated with the cowardly party in a dispute since the man in question buys his goodwill and protection by promising to foster Olaf and make him his heir. Melkorka, who is a woman of royal distinction, protests; Hoskuld placates her by explaining what a good arrangement it is for their son.

Hoskuld is thus a man who gets involved in the edges of many conflicts – and sometimes further in – who indeed does his best to initiate them. But positive forces around him – his wife's prudence and his brother's patience – prevent these conflicts from having tragic consequences. He is praised when mentioned, if he is spoken of directly. He is described as "a handsome and accomplished youth" (c. 7, V 6) when he is introduced, and finally, of his death it is said that he "was greatly mourned" (c. 26, V 36).

But his behaviour, in contrast to that of his brother and wife – and unlike that of those who will be discussed below – tells a different story. The difference in qualities between the two brothers is a constitutive element in their story. And even though the brothers are reconciled, conflicts are not removed from the surface of the earth – nor from the family – by Hoskuld's death.

Conflicts Contained
Two of Hoskuld's many children comprise the corresponding pairing in the next generation: Olaf Peacock, who is the son of his concubine Melkorka, and Thorleik, who is the oldest of his legitimate children. The competitive relationship between the mothers repeats itself in a different yet recognisable form in the sons. But the conflict never develops into open strife. This is due to Olaf Peacock, a peace-maker and conciliator like the great Njal, whom he resembles in more than one way.

The now familiar source of conflict – strife over inheritance – is present from the moment that the two half-brothers take centre stage, at Hoskuld's death bed. Thorleik denies his dying father's right to make his illegitimate son Olaf equally entitled to inherit with the other brothers. So the expiring Hoskuld asks to be allowed at least to give Olaf a gift from the estate before it is divided. Thorleik, like the third brother, Bard, agrees, but immediately afterwards, unlike his legitimate brother, retracts his witnessed agreement. Olaf meanwhile openly insists on what he has grounds to consider his right.

This is the beginning of "the coolness which arises between Thorleik and Olaf" (c. 26). This enmity and the circuitous way in which it unfolds is the subject of the central portion of the three-part saga.

Olaf's first conciliatory transaction with his brother consists in his offer to take Thorleik's son Bolli as his foster son. Such an offer implies, according to saga conventions, a declaration of social inferiority: anyone who took another's son as a foster child thereby conceded that he occupied a lower social ranking; Olaf reminds Thorleik of this quite openly (c. 27). Thorleik accepts the offer.

Olaf resembles Njal in his being a peace-maker. He resembles him also in that his very efforts to achieve reconciliation contain the seeds of new and unexpected conflicts. Olaf becomes reconciled with Thorleik by taking in his son. But in doing so he brings together the two cousins Kjartan and Bolli and lays the groundwork for the competition that nourishes the saga's greatest conflict, which Olaf himself is powerless to control. This breaks out in the saga's last and longest section, the story of the "third" generation.

But the conflicts in the "second" generation Olaf is still able – almost – to control. After the reconciliation Thorleik no longer turns his hostility directly against Olaf, but against his counterpart in the "first" generation, the temperate Hrut. When I use a commendatory adjective to describe the latter – and thereby take a position in the conflict – I am not employing a reader's rights to arbitrary judgement. It is the saga's narrator who, in his typical indirect way, guides the reader to this view.

A man challenges Thorleik's honour – the issue is a horse deal – and later takes the law into his own hands. Hrut intervenes and kills the man, but this causes Thorleik to think his honour challenged by Hrut.

> Thorleik responded angrily and felt that he had been put to shame, while Hrut thought he had done him a real service. (c. 37, V 53)

Here two interpretations are in conflict. How are we to form a judgement? It is not necessary to seek out the non-existing surviving historical sources and conjecture about the social morality of the time. The text, which is a coherent whole, speaks for itself:

> Hrut was over eighty when he killed Eldgrim, and gained a great deal of respect as a result of the deed. (c. 37, V 53)

Here the saga world's highest court passes sentence: the anonymous collective that bestows reputation or its opposite. Thorleik is in the wrong when he meditates on how to insult Hrut for his performance; society is in the right when it calls it honourable.

Thorleik's whims are so extreme that even Hrut loses patience. But it is Olaf he turns to on the day this finally happens, and the two men of peace united suffice to prevent Thorleik's provocations from splitting the family. Thorleik exits the narrative without ever bringing about the open combat he has been working towards the entire time.

Hrut and Olaf are two variants of a basic type in the saga.

Hrut's peacemaking function expresses itself through his *respect for the law*. If, in his struggle with Hoskuld, his well-motivated decision to take matters into his own hands comes late and reluctantly, it is because he has pursued his case according to the provisions of the law for so long. And when he has his first collision with Thorleik, he again prosecutes his case according to the law (c. 25). It goes against him. He acquiesces and abides by its ruling.

Olaf goes further. He does his best to forestall the disorder that threatens. When the quarrel over inheritance between him and Thorleik has come to a sort of conclusion, he goes a step further than is necessary for the moment: he humbles himself by offering to foster Thorleik's son. The idea is that present action will prevent future difficulty. The same notion may be behind Olaf's remarkable behaviour at his daughter's divorce.

Thurid married Geirmund much against her father Olaf's wish. Geirmund is in fact a cantankerous fellow (*ódældar-madr*, c. 29) and such a man constitutes a threat to society. The marriage develops as Olaf had anticipated. But when he is consulted about its dissolution, he becomes more non-committal. Suddenly he has no strong opinions and – what is most striking – when the divorce takes place according to the economic stipulations that the husband alone has laid down, the humbled father-in-law bestows the gift of a ship on the departing man as a preventive measure against future troubles: if another has committed an injustice against one, one should eat humble pie to avoid future recurrences. As the word used to designate him at this point indicates, Olaf is a *samningar-madr* (c. 30), a conciliator.

But he has here reached the outer limits of his conciliatory efforts. Fraternal strife and the struggle for authority between men, these he has hitherto been able to deal with. Some lands lie there neglected and unclaimed, because there is some question as to whether he is able to seize them, exorcise a ghost, and incorporate them within the bounds of society (c. 24). In this little story we have an emblem of the peacemaker's function: to draw the disordered, which is a menace to society, under the control of law and order. But only where no erotic impulses or humiliations are involved can he fulfill this function without having to give up. He can bestow gifts on his departing son-in-law and speak mildly to him. But he cannot undo what has happened to his rejected daughter in this case. The traces of this continue in the family in the form of the sword Leg-biter, which will later cause a wound that cannot be healed.

The sword gains symbolic prominence in the narrative when Thurid snatches it away from the ill-tempered Geirmund shortly before his departure, knowing that it is his most treasured possession. And she gives it to her foster-brother Bolli, who will in due course use it to kill his own foster-brother Kjartan. There is no causal linkage between Thurid's humiliation and the humiliation which later leads to Bolli's slaying of Kjartan. The connection is established symbolically.

The meaning of the narrative sequence just mentioned is to shape the reader's understanding of the kind of humiliations that are involved, the seat of the compulsions that were in play, when Olaf's peacemaking at last comes up short: erotic competition and erotic rejection instigate the form of savagery which is the only quite ungovernable threat to order according to the philosophy of existence that underlies *Laxdœla Saga*.

Here it is just Thurid's impotent effort at vengeance against her husband. It has no consequences beyond the symbolic and at the same time practical one that it introduces into the family the sword by which a man will later strike down his brother.

It is at this time that Olaf dreams that he will lose his most beloved son (c. 31). And it is at this point that Gudrun enters the saga as the agent of the chaos that threatens the social order (c. 32). Everything is prepared for the story of the saga's "third" generation in which the philosophy of the saga will present itself most clearly.

Irresolvable Conflict at Last
By the time Bolli kills his cousin, foster brother, and best friend Kjartan, Olaf has made seven attempts at arranging a reconciliation in the conflict. There is no clearer way of showing that he, who has hitherto achieved so much as a mediator, has reached the limit of his ability.

When things go as they do, it is not because Kjartan or Bolli have suddenly changed character and become men of violence. The compulsion that drives the conflict does not come from them, but from the pattern that has involuntarily been introduced into the narrative.

As boys the two foster brothers are inseparable:

Kjartan was the leader of Olaf's sons, and he and Bolli were very close. Kjartan never went anywhere without Bolli at his side. (c. 39, V 57)

From which it follows – without actually being said – that Bolli was on hand also when Kjartan made his many visits to Gudrun, a young woman though already twice married and a widow. So the two young men had both met and come to know this exciting woman, when they together – ever inseparable – set out on the customary voyage to Norway. In Norway the first crack in their relationship occurs.

Kjartan shows his accomplishment in a swimming contest against none other than the young king Olaf Tryggvason. Bolli lacks both the desire and the ability. Kjartan earns the king's highest favour and becomes a close friend of his sister. Bolli travels to Iceland and proposes to Gudrun. She accepts, though she and Kjartan parted with an agreement that could be called a quasi-engagement. Hence the fatal fact that Kjartan and Gudrun fail to marry.

What is happening in this narrative segment is the interlinking of the urge to excel and the erotic impulse which creates a catastrophic, irresolvable combination. Consider how each of the two young people, who appear to be destined for each other, become parted (c. 40).

Gudrun asks Kjartan's permission to travel with him when he tells her of his imminent voyage to Norway. He refuses, but asks in return that she wait for him for three years. In repayment for his refusal she denies *his* request. They are equally attracted to each other – and equally proud. Bolli fails in comparison to Kjartan when they confront the same challenge: Olaf Tryggvasson. In return he is able to avenge himself by getting home first and winning Gudrun with the story that Kjartan has been pursuing the king's sister.

The saga does not present Bolli as a liar in this passage – on the contrary it lends his account a certain degree of reliability, though one is left wondering quite how much. The saga does not deal with villains and heroes, but with basic impulses that struggle within the individual. And, it is important to observe, first and foremost with the outer, social consequences of this struggle. In this it distinguishes itself most clearly from the classical or romantic treatment of the same eternal struggle, for example in Racine's *Phaedre* or in Oehlenschlager's *Kjartan and Gudrun*.

The pattern to be observed in Kjartan's and Gudrun's parting conversation, covers the rest of the saga's climactic events.

Bolli marries Gudrun after showing his inferiority to Kjartan (c. 43); Gudrun marries Bolli in the same circumstances. Kjartan comes home to Iceland, finds himself to have been humiliated by the two and marries Hrefna (c. 45); at a feast for the two families, Kjartan humiliates Gudrun by placing Hrefna on the high-seat and Gudrun responds by causing precious possessions to be taken from Kjartan (c. 46); now it is Kjartan's turn, Gudrun and Bolli and their household are locked in their farmhouse for three days so that they have to relieve themselves indoors (c. 47); and so at length the escalating enmity comes to a climax and Bolli is almost forced by Gudrun to take Kjartan's life.

We might possibly interpret this distressing course of events solely as the result of the urge to excel – together with the pride and sensitivity to humiliation that accompanies it – and also as a variant of the conflict we encounter so often in the sagas of Icelanders involving solely men – but only if we ignore the context in which it occurs.

The saga narrative has related numerous conflicts between men up to this point, but the conflicts between such major characters have not been insoluble. Conciliators like Hrut and Olaf have always been able to prevent the worst. For the first time now, when the humiliations visited on characters include an erotic dimension, the danger becomes unavoidable, even though Olaf tries harder to forestall it than at any other time in the saga. Peace makers can deal with boundary disputes and inheritance squabbles; confronted with erotic outrages their powers fail them.

The Pattern
The threat that the erotic poses to the social order is a motif that emerges very early in the saga. It enters already when Thorgerd, mother of the main narrative's "first" generation, marries for a second time (c. 7). But things continue to proceed lawfully and society therefore has the means – laws – to cope with the consequences that flow from it.

The behaviour of the contestants tends to degenerate as the story progresses.

The curious sub-plot already mentioned (c. 14-16) about a killing occasioned by a trifling disagreement between two minor characters can only be understood as an omen of this decline – with the result that, like so much else in this carefully structured saga, it only begins to make sense when one has finished reading the saga. Thorgerd remarries after being widowed and after obtaining her family's approval; three generations later Gudrun remarries after having obtained a divorce on fabricated grounds. Kjartan is killed in an ambush to be sure, but the conflict that precedes his death is open; the killing of Thorgils, who is a victim of an act of counter-vengeance in the third generation, takes place after a settlement has been arranged:

> Thorgils had begun counting out silver when Audgisl Thorarinsson passed by and, just as Thorgils said ten, Audgisl swung at him; everyone thought they could hear his head say eleven as it flew off his body. (c. 67, V 103)

There is a similar decline in the series of peacemakers in the saga: we have already met the *samningarmenn* of the first two generations, Hrut and Olaf; the third generation also has its own, Snorri Godi, who achieves the saga's final peace settlement (c. 71). But he is also the man behind the loathsome assassination of Thorgils!

It is not difficult to continue the enumeration of such parallels which demonstrate the ebbing of honourable motive as time passes. Distinctions of worth cut across each of the saga's generations as we began by noting, between Hrut and Hoskuld, between Olaf and Thorleik, between Kjartan and Bolli; equally important distinctions run lengthwise through the narrative, between the successive generations. The saga treats of a decay which escalates with the growing failure of the law to channel erotic drives.

However, this is not a story of dissolution pure and simple. It does not end on the note that the ugly murder of Thorgils strikes. Chaos introduces dissolution into the social world of the saga, but order springs up anew in the end. To understand its place we must return to the first chapters of the saga.

The first, as yet unmentioned, person who emerges from the throng as a major character is Unn, Hoskuld and Hrut's great-grandmother, one of the original settlers of Iceland, incarnation of the values upon which the initial social order was constructed. As the saga-teller writes, in one of the saga's exceptions to the rule that qualities should never be explicitly specified, she is "a paragon among women" (c. 4). She sets out for Iceland like her brothers with a splendid following and takes possession of an enormous tract of land, so large that all Laxardal, whose ownership many of the characters in the unfolding story must later divide, is the dowry she bestows in just one of the many marriages she sponsors. This sponsoring is her primary role in the saga. Once it is accomplished and she has announced her testament during the wedding festivity, she is found the next day "sitting upright among the pillows, dead" (c. 7, V 6).

From first to last she is a person associated with order. Scarcely has she appeared in the text when she becomes a grandmother, the head of her family, a stage of life at which disruptive erotic urges only seldom intervene and create disorder in the family. She creates the foundation for the lawful family connections in the next two generations, puts her home and lands in order and exits the saga, sitting upright.

The order and dignity she represents are lost once and for all with her departure. But they reappear at the saga's end in another guise.

Christianity is introduced part way through the narrative. Kjartan is converted to the new faith under the influence of Olaf Tryggvason and carries it with him to Iceland. This faith contributes as little to averting his pitiable death as to preventing the decay that sets in afterwards in the form of intrigues and secret murder. It plays no role at all until the very end. But then it certainly enters into the central narrative structure. For when Gudrun has lived through everything, when she has married for the fourth time and for the third time been widowed, when she has at length reached Unn's grandmotherly age,

> Gudrun became very religious. She was the first Icelandic woman to learn the Psalter and spent long period in the church praying at night. (c. 76, V 117)

If Unn was the last of the noble settlers, Gudrun in her turn becomes the first nun and anchoress in Iceland (c. 78).

Dignity is re-established, order is reintroduced, the circle closed. Unn and the aged Gudrun function in *Laxdœla Saga* as Hamlet's father and the young Fortinbras function in Hamlet: the two fixed points between which chaos and degradation reign for a time.

If we consider the relationship between royal power and the free-men, and the mutual rivalry between the two groups, to be a major problem in the sagas of Icelanders, the two sagas examined so far must seem to be the opposite to one another.

In *Egil's Saga* all evils seem at first glance to come from the king. In *Laxdœla Saga* royal power also creates problems: had Kjartan not been so impressed by the life among royalty one can imagine that he would not have remained so long in Norway and perhaps he would have arrived home in Iceland in time to prevent the misbegotten marriage between Gudrun and Bolli. But such considerations lead nowhere, for it is clear that royal power in all its splendour beguiles the story-teller as much as it does the hero. King Olaf is the Norwegian counterpart of the Icelandic Kjartan. And Christianization, which lays the groundwork for the new order, is the result of royal power.

The complete story of the saga – and the role of royal power in it – is epitomized in the three swords that appear in it.

Leg-biter, of which we have already spoken, enters into the family through a reckless erotic connection and quickly undermines the marriage between Geirmund and Thurid. From there it passes to another reckless relationship, that between Bolli and his wife Gudrun; Gudrun places it in Bolli's hand to use against Kjartan.

Yet another sword of vengeance turns up towards the saga's conclusion, the sword Skofnung, whose nature is so dark that "the sun must not be allowed to shine on its hilt, nor may it be drawn in the presence of women" (c. 57, V 89). It is introduced by Thorkel who later becomes Gudrun's fourth husband.

But the power of vengeance to solve conflicts seems to have passed: the sword does not function according to its purpose (c. 58). As the text makes explicit it is not until the avenger Thorkel is drowned, with the sword Skofnung aboard his ship, that Gudrun can enter into the new order.

Skofnung is recovered and taken ashore from the lost ship and is passed on to Thorkel's and Gudrun's son Gellir, whose task in the saga's conclusion is to effect the removal of the sword from the story. The origins of Skofnung lie in the distant past. It was taken out of Rolf Kraki's grave in Roskilde. Through its part in the occurrences in *Laxdæla Saga* it partakes in the decay as times goes by. At Gellir's side it completes the circle from the oldest times to the new. Gellir travels to Denmark – he "had taken Skofnung abroad with him" – is baptised and buried in Roskilde the place where the sword came from, which has now become a Christian holy site. And of Skofnung it is said that "the sword was never recovered after that" (c. 78, V 119, 120).

The third sword is Skofnung's opposite. It is referred to as the King's-gift because Kjartan received it from the king. It belongs to the daylight. But at the crucial moment when Bolli kills Kjartan with the sword Leg-biter, Kjartan does not have it with him. From Leg-biter to Skofnung is the time of the destructive function of the swords.

The King's-gift does not reappear. But Leg-biter takes over its role. When it turned up originally it was described as "lacking any silver" and with a "sharp blade" (c. 29). In the end (c. 77) when it hangs by the side of Bolli Bollason, it has a golden hilt and a grip wound about with gold. Einar Ólafur Sveinsson, who prepared the edition that is the basis for this reading, has recorded his puzzlement at these two irreconcilable descriptions. One can only praise and thank philology, which prompts philologists to restore texts faithfully, resisting emendations but recording puzzlement in the foot-notes; without it literary analyses would be impossible.

For the apparent discrepancy has indeed an inner meaning. The style and appearance of royal power go hand in hand with the re-establishment of dignity and order caused by Christianization; therefore the transformed Leg-biter can be used as accompaniment to the transformation of the human beings that takes place towards the end. Leg-biter's role as destroyer is over once the story of Gudrun and Kjartan and Bolli has drawn to a close.

If *Egil's Saga* and *Laxdæla Saga* may be seen to take opposite positions in their views of royal power, they are conversely similar in their deepest interest: what are the forces that destroy order in society? Similar too are the answers the two sagas return to this question.

It is no misfortune when people marry one another without being urged by passion. On the contrary it is most usual in the sagas. The crucial point is what happens once a marriage has taken place. Things can proceed as they do with Herjolf and Thorgerd, who marry first and later fall in love with one another. It may also be the case, as it is with Hoskuld and Jorunn or with Olaf and Thorgerd, that nothing is said of the second stage of these love relationships, the love relationship which later times customarily treat as stage one: that of falling in love. Whether or not that happens is of little concern to the saga. The saga does not care about quiet languishment; what the saga cares about are social consequences.

Ill luck first enters the moment that urges arise that contravene established conduct and it is first to be clearly observed the moment these urges become so strong – or their agents so weak – that they lead to *actions* that contravene the conduct that families agree to through marriage contracts. And when at last these urges fuse together with the impulse to excel, nothing can withstand the ill luck. When law can no longer harness the urges, the worst happens. "I behaved worst to the man I loved most," says Gudrun as she reflects on her life.

To show patience and turn the other cheek may be a true Christian virtue. But the character of Olaf Peacock shows that it does not help.

It is not this form of Christianity that is found in the sagas. The place that Christianity occupies in the construction of the sagas is as an ordering force which by means of its moral regeneration and chastity can re-establish the order and dignity that prevailed when the land was first settled, but which got lost when it became inhabited. *Laxdæla Saga* is the Icelandic myth of creation, fall and redemption. And the most dangerous sin is to give in to one's impulses and disregard the social order.

Below we will see this theme taken up and explored in *Njal's Saga*. But first we must take one step backwards in time.

CHAPTER 2

FORERUNNERS

Kormak's Saga, Bjorn's Saga, Eyrbyggja Saga

The pattern we have now observed in two sagas of Icelanders and later will see in many more is by no means universal.

We do not know the exact date when any of the sagas of Icelanders made its appearance, but thanks to extensive research it has become possible to advance defensible conjectures that give us some idea at least of their sequence. More will be said about the basis of these conjectures in my penultimate chapter.

The vast majority of sagas of Icelanders were written in the thirteenth century. *Egil's Saga* is considered to have been written in the century's first decades, before or perhaps about the year 1230. *Laxdœla Saga* is supposed to have appeared sometime later, but before, probably not long before, 1280. These two works are among the masterworks of saga writing; most of the remaining classic sagas of Icelanders should probably be placed in the period between these two dates – always in accordance with the arguments and indicators that have been established thus far.

To the early part of the period of saga-writing, contemporary with or slightly predating *Egil's Saga*, belong such sagas as *Kormak's Saga*, *Bjorn's Saga* and *Eyrbyggja Saga*; the first two are very likely older, the last may also be. A reading of these three pre-classical sagas will help us to illuminate the first two sagas we have examined. Once again we find that erotic impulse plays a role in these three older sagas, but the interest that they take in its consequences distinguishes them from the classical sagas.

It is *Kormak's Saga* that most clearly casts into relief what I have called the second pattern – the significance of erotic impulse not confined to two persons only but affecting an entire, albeit small, community. For *Kormak's Saga*, which deals more clearly and consistently with love than any other saga of Icelanders, confines its attention to only two characters – essentially indeed only to one.

The prelude is short in comparison to those in *Laxdœla Saga* and *Egil's Saga*. The centralization of the Norwegian monarchy, the emigration, and the two generations before the hero are dealt with on a single page, contributing little to the saga apart from the establishment of the time-frame. Already by the second chapter we meet Kormak and already by the third Kormak meets Steingerd, at which point the course of his life is determined.

To be sure, it takes a little while before it becomes clear that he will never be united with Steingerd, though he will love her at a distance until his death. But the conditions that will produce this situation are present from the beginning. For Kormak is no man of action, nor is he a poet *and* a man of action like Egil; Kormak is simply a poet.

The first he sees of Steingerd is her feet, which are sticking out from under a wooden table. It is enough to cause him to break out into a love verse. Next he sees her eyes; this produces three verses. Then he hears her speak – more verses – and then he sees all of her: more verses still. Kormak has fallen in love, or in any case become a love-poet.

Steingerd's father is not much in favour of the connection. He hires two men to kill Kormak. But Kormak anticipates the attack and kills them. This infuriates the young men's mother. "There's nothing more likely than that you'll arrange things so that I'm compelled to flee from the district, with my sons unatoned for; but this is how I'll pay you back for it: you will never enjoy Steingerd's love" (c. 5, I 187). And since she is a witch no further grounds are required for things to go as she has predicted. It is worth noting that the magic works in familiar ways: Kormak fails to win Steingerd simply because he loses his desire for her at the very moment he could have her.

Despite the bold attempt to get rid of the suitor, Steingerd's father finally yields under his pressure. Kormak and Steingerd become engaged. But on the appointed wedding day Kormak fails to appear and sends no explanation. So Steingerd is married to a rowdy old widower, Bersi, at which point Kormak's desire is rekindled.

He gets hold of a magic sword, Skofnung, which shares its name and characteristics with the sword in *Laxdœla Saga*. With this the path to Steingerd again becomes clear, even if this time the path lies over Bersi's corpse.

But now we get a clearer explanation than before about what happens when Kormak fails to seize an opportunity. Skofnung does not work, for Kormak breaks the rules that bind him to the sword; he does so in fact just after he has got them memorized. He tries to draw the sword but a woman – his mother – gazes on it and allows the sun to shine on its hilt (c. 9). Given the memory attributed to the saga hero, this cannot be blamed on forgetfulness. What we come to understand is that magic seizes a person's very will causing him to *want* something other than what he believes himself to want. Consequently Bersi is not killed in their duel.

Steingerd divorces herself from the husband forced upon her. But that does not help either; we hear nothing further about Kormak before Steingerd is married to another man.

With this Kormak's love flares up again. He seeks out Steingerd and asks the newly-married woman to sew him a shirt, which in the sagas always serves as a love token. She does him the kindness of saying no, which contributes mightily to his love; the verses come tumbling out anew. Kormak travels to Norway with his brother and the farther away he gets, the more loudly he sings of his love. He comes home and spends a night alone with Steingerd, although on the other side of a wooden screen – or bed board, as "brík" should probably be translated – as his poem of the passing of the night recounts (c. 19).

Once again he travels abroad. This time Steingerd pursues him followed by her second husband, and Kormak and Steingerd take turns humiliating one another and following one another.

When Kormak has rescued Steingerd from some robbers, her husband at last thinks that he too must do something; he proposes to Steingerd that she can have Kormak. It might seem to fit the pattern almost too well, if it were Kormak who said no yet again – one loses track which time this would be. But such is not the case, even if Hans E. Kinck happens to say so in his article on the saga. It is Steingerd who refuses.

Nevertheless Kinck is right in the conclusion that he draws, for there are, as we have seen, instances enough to build on in the story. The saga deals with a hero who loves violently, but recoils from possession. In other words it deals with a common literary phenomenon: "the disappearance of the individual and his replacement by the type."

> It is a skald who expresses his love in a poem to her. Through the lines of his intricate *dróttkvætt* she is transformed from the beloved into the object of song, into a model. In this resides the central feature of this love relationship, which is the tragedy of the genius and the human being. (Kinck 1921, 76)

In the poetry of the nineteenth century, to encounter this problem would not merit comment: during that period any number of books devote themselves to it. But it is rather surprising to find so clear and exemplary a treatment of it at the beginning of the period of saga writing – to which *Kormak's Saga* belongs, if the dating of recent philologists is preferred to that of Finnur Jónsson. There has been a tendency to consider this saga side by side with a romance like *Tristram's Saga*, which was translated into Old Norse in 1226. The two works share the absence of union and the passions that swell during – indeed *because of* – separation. But *Kormak's Saga* is alone in linking erotic abstinence with poetic gifts. It failed to initiate any tradition in Iceland.

It is possible that Kinck's fine interpretation depends too much upon the fact that Kormak is a poet. The favourite problem of the nineteenth century may have been projected onto the medieval text. The source of the error could be that it is the rule, rather than the exception, that the high points in sagas coalesce in skaldic verses, whether by the hero himself or by another.

In any case another viewpoint than Kinck's will guide the discussion here. According to this view too *Kormak's Saga* should be treated as standing alone, without predecessors and predating the composition of the classical sagas.

Kormak's Saga is short of killings and violent occurrences. At the beginning Kormak slays a man, but no blood vengeance comes of this. Kormak engages in a duel with Steingerd's husband, but this *holmgang* results in nothing more than a scratched thumb. In addition Kormak kills two persons of no importance, neither of whom is avenged in blood.

In other words the conflict sets no avalanche in motion. It fails to affect significantly the relations between groups of people. It has no disturbing impact on the order of the small community involved. The only person disturbed by it, apart from Kormak, is Steingerd.

Kinck sketches the psychological drama he imagines must have played itself out in her, and reproaches the saga writer for not describing it. But it is more important to observe the consequences of what he *has* done than to reproach him for what he has *not* done.

The drama is concentrated wholly and entirely in Kormak. Steingerd is a foil for the action being played out in him. She may well have entered into her first marriage, with Bersi, out of spite and humiliation. What matters is that it has none of the consequences of Gudrun's similar match with Bolli. At a suitable opportunity Steingerd divorces herself from her husband and remarries in accordance with her family's advice and "with no protest from her" (c. 17, I 207).

By this means the exterior social order is reconstituted in the family, which has been so disturbed by Kormak's feelings. All that remains are these feelings. Kormak's ill-fated romance is without social consequence. And that is the crucial difference between the love narrative in *Kormak's Saga*, and that in *Laxdæla Saga* or *Egil's Saga*.

Bjorn's Saga, or, more properly *The Saga of Bjorn Champion of the Hitardal People,* is a different kind of precursor to the classic saga of Icelanders and probably dates from about 1220. In this saga it is the social consequences, the quarrels, that absorb almost all the attention, while the love complications that occur in the saga share no significant connections with them.

Bjorn and his adversary Thord do battle throughout most of the saga. Theodore M. Andersson (1967) has calculated that two-thirds of the narrative is dedicated to the hostile encounters between the two men, which number eighteen altogether. The presentation of characters in the saga's opening is strikingly similar to that in *Laxdæla Saga*; it is for this reason, in fact, that the differences between them have not escaped notice.

Bjorn falls in love with Oddny and travels abroad for three years. Thord, who has also been traveling abroad, comes home first and tells Oddny that Bjorn is dead. She temporises until three years have passed; afterwards she accepts Thord's suit and marries him. Bjorn has survived and comes to spend the rest of his life battling against Thord.

A similar sort of summary might be sketched for the story Kjartan and Gudrun and Bolli. But if we move beyond summary we will observe how the similarities fail.

Thord is presented as an evil man from the beginning of the saga. "He seemed to be mocking and spiteful to everyone he considered himself a match for" (c. 1, I 255), including Bjorn, who in this connection, emerges as the good hero. This is the first difference between the two sagas. From it all the other differences follow.

Thord and Bjorn become friends of a kind while abroad. Bjorn sends Thord home to Oddny with his greetings. But the shiftless fellow takes the liberty of adding that Bjorn has bequeathed Oddny to him, if he should die (c. 3). And when Thord later hears reports that Bjorn has been wounded, he tells the bearer of the report to announce that Bjorn is dead. By this strategy Thord manages to marry Oddny.

What has occurred, and the saga writer is quite unequivocal about it, is a swindle and a fraud. After this Oddny retreats into the background. She does not incite either of the two men during their protracted feud. Only towards the end of the story, when she swoons at the news of Bjorn's death and succumbs to incurable illness (c. 33), is one reminded that she too is an injured party.

The essential difference between the two related stories in the *Laxdœla Saga* and *Bjorn's Saga* is therefore this: while the quarrel between Kjartan and Bolli follows after the emergence of unlawful impulses, between Bjorn and Thord the situation is reversed – what Thord does to Bjorn in stealing away his bride is an expression of his wickedness, a wickedness accepted as a given, for which no explanation is provided. The conceptual universe presented in *Bjorn's Saga* is simple: strife in this world is a result of the existence of good men and bad, who simply happen to be one or the other.

At one point Thord and Bjorn allow the king to arbitrate their quarrel (c. 8). He judges that Thord's theft of Bjorn's woman should be set against Bjorn's theft of Thord's goods. That no peace results from this settlement may be thought to point forward towards the more complex analysis of strife in the classical sagas: strife cannot be eliminated from the world by means of a monetary settlement. The constitutive elements of what will later appear as the second pattern in the sagas of Icelanders are already in place. But this composition belongs still to the preliminary stages: the theft of the woman can be replaced by other offences – and in fact follows *after* other offences – as a simple link in a series. It could be dispensed with or replaced by some other wickedness without the saga falling to pieces. To covet your neighbour's ass or your neighbour's wife has the same consequences. Were the classical sagas constructed in this particular way, there would be no reason to talk of a second pattern.

Kormak's Saga directs its attention inwards towards the psychic consequences of unrealized love. *Bjorn's Saga* directs its attention outwards towards the conflicts that no reconciliation can resolve. The classic Icelandic sagas had not yet emerged to pursue the analysis to the point that these two viewpoints are combined into a single design.

And so to the third preliminary run, *Eyrbyggja Saga,* or *The Saga of the People of Eyri*. It too is thought to be early, before 1200 according to Finnur Jónsson, a scholar who favoured early dates for the entire saga corpus; from before 1222 according to Einar Ólafur Sveinsson; not before 1240 – because not before *Laxdæla Saga* – according to a third opinion held by some philologists. The uncertainty as regards its date of composition is thus rather greater than for the two other sagas discussed in this chapter. Irrespective of whether the first, second, or third view is correct, all are agreed in seeing *Eyrbyggja Saga* as a better source of cultural history and by the same token as a less unified narrative than most of the central sagas of Icelanders. It might be that, in terms of chronology, it does not belong among the precursors to the classical sagas, it nevertheless exhibits the features of the precursors. Also in this, possibly early, saga the second pattern can be glimpsed beginning to take shape. But nothing more than that.

In the above-mentioned study of the sagas of Icelanders (160f) Theodore M. Andersson is able to count in all ten separate narratives in *Eyrbyggja Saga*, each of which could form the basis of a separate saga. But instead they are all linked together into a long, rather disconnected narrative. Let us examine one of these narrative links (c. 25-28).

Two Swedish berserks, Halli and his brother, voyage out to Iceland, not because they want to but persuaded by the Icelander Vermund who in return has promised not to refuse any wish of theirs that he has the power to satisfy. After they arrive in Iceland, Halli wants Vermund's help in arranging a good marriage. Vermund refuses, and nothing bad happens as long as the desire remains only an abstract one. In the meantime Vermund proceeds to hand the berserks over to his brother Styr, at which point the desire takes concrete form: Halli wants to marry Styr's daughter.

Styr also tries to wriggle out the obligation. But he realizes that in this kind of situation a simple refusal will not suffice. He turns for advice to the character who more than any other dominates the saga, Snorri the Godi. What Snorri's plan is we do not hear. Rather we see it put into action.

Styr sets as a condition that Halli perform a difficult task – clear a road – if he is indeed to have his daughter. In the meantime Styr prepares a warm bath-house for the berserks, in which he slays them. Then Snorri the Godi appears, once the deed has been done, and himself marries Styr's daughter.

This is the kind of behaviour we find in the middle section, the section depicting social decay, in sagas like *Laxdæla Saga* or *Njal's Saga* that contain the complete mythic cycle. As a matter of fact we recognise Snorri the Godi's behaviour because he acts similarly in *Laxdæla Saga*, and it is this kind of connection between suitors, marriage, and lawlessness, that sets in motion the lasting shockwaves in the great sagas. In *Eyrbyggja Saga* no consequences ensue. The saga hastens along to other episodes in which Snorri is involved.

A foreign body has intruded into the social organism and been pushed out again. Considering the kind of foreign body – a berserk and moreover a Swede – the saga writer can afford to take a liberal view of the means used to expel him. A concern for the connection between society's decay and morality has yet to be established. The ingredients are there but they are not yet interacting.

These sagas can be considered as a preparation whether they arose – as *Kormak's Saga* almost certainly did – before the classical sagas, or were written – as *Eyrbyggja Saga* may have been – a good way into the classical period, if by the word preparation one understands a simpler treatment irrespective of when it was composed: the great sagas extend and deepen the analysis carried out in these works.

One could lengthen the list. *The Saga of the People of Vopnafjord* is shaped according to the pattern in *Bjorn's Saga*, although it is considered to be later than the other sagas in this chapter, from about 1230. In *The Saga of the Sworn Brothers,* Thorgeir deals with the scuffles of men and Thormod Kolbrunskald deals with the women; there is no connection between their two spheres of action beyond the extrinsic fact that the two heroes happen to be sworn brothers. In the same saga it happens that a man plays around with a young woman and the parents are opposed, unless he intends to marry her. In yet another pre-classical saga, *The Saga of Hallfred the Troublesome Poet*, this is similarly a recurrent problem. It sounds very familiar – even Victorian.

In the classical *Gisli's Saga*, a high point in the corpus of saga literature, this problem is related for the first time to its social consequences; around it occurs the clash of two conventions, society is shifting. With *Gisli's Saga* we have arrived back at the focal point of classical saga composition.

CHAPTER 3

THE SECOND PATTERN: BETWEEN TWO SOCIETIES

Gisli Sursson's Saga

When we are reading sagas whose story is slender and violent – *The Saga of Bjorn Champion of the Hitardal People*, for example – we may sometimes wonder what attitude the saga writer in fact wants us to adopt with regard to actions that we would consider injustices and murders. If we proceed to a saga like *Gisli Sursson's Saga* or, as it is known more simply, *Gisli's Saga*, our doubts disappear again. Here our interest is not captured by the murders as such, rather our attention is directed towards the causes that lead a good man to become a killer or to be killed himself. Both things happened to one of the saga literature's greatest creations, Gisli Sursson. The question is why?

Gisli's best friend – his wife's brother – is murdered by Gisli's own brother or brother-in-law; Gisli murders the brother-in-law – his sister's husband – and is himself murdered through the instigation of his sister, who later makes a vain attempt to kill Gisli's slayer, though she herself had instigated his action. Matters could scarcely go worse, but worst of all there is no scoundrel to be pointed to, no Thord on whom the blame can be heaped. Blame must be laid on the interplay between forces within individual persons – forces which are not in themselves evil – and the rules that govern the interactions between persons – rules that also are without fault in themselves. The trouble is that these two elements no longer match. Each individual wants to protect his own life and the lives of his family. The rules for the commerce among people, rules to support the family and avenge wrongdoing, have the same goal. Nevertheless, the result of the specific occurrences is the opposite: people perish and the family suffers dissolution.

If one knows the story one can already guess in the prologue what must go wrong. The first time one reads the book, one's suspicions are aroused at the same time that Gisli's are, by the unlucky occurrences that come to pass during the spring thing, when the saga's four principal characters – Gisli and his wife's brother Vestein on the one side, and Gisli's brother Thorkel and their sister's husband Thorgrim on the other – decide to enter into blood-brotherhood. Normally there should be no need for such a pact, for the four are the best of friends. But the wise Gest has said that their friendship will scarcely survive for three years. And Gisli, a cautious man, has heard the prediction and proposes to his three friends that they do something to frustrate it. Thus the blood-brotherhood ceremony.

But such an action cannot avert the problem. What Gisli achieves with his proposal is rather to bring the problem to light:

> But as they clasped hands, Thorgrim said, "I will have enough trouble to deal with if I so bind myself to Thorkel and Gisli, my brothers-in-law, but I bear no obligation to Vestein" – and he quickly withdrew his hand (c. 6, II 7)

With this everything is lost. The fissures, of which only the second-sighted Gest had previously had forebodings, have become clearly visible. The four friends have become two separate pairs: Gisli and Vestein, Thorkel and Thorgrim. But we are given no explanation for the split.

The jealousies we hear about later may be thought to provide this explanation. It appears (c. 9) that Thorkel's wife Asgerd nourishes a silent love for Vestein and has long done so. On the same occasion we come to learn that Gisli's wife Aud has had a relationship with Thorgrim, before she was married to Gisli. This too can be supposed to have contributed to the division of the four friends into two pairs.

However, the two similar triangles function more to reveal the differences between the two brothers, Gisli and Thorkel, than the likenesses between them. The literary strategy employed here had to await nineteenth-century impressionism to be put to serious use again by prose writers. By placing two characters in similar situations and showing how differently they react, the saga writer avoids having to assert anything about the characters' differences; instead they can be allowed simply to reveal themselves. This is one of the finest examples of showing rather than telling. What happens is this.

Thorkel overhears a conversation between the two women in which their forgotten or hidden feelings are revealed. Already there is a difference between the two women. Asgerd does not deny that she continues to love a man other than her husband. Aud conversely can state that she has not had any relationship behind Gisli's back.

And the difference between the two women manifests itself still more clearly when it becomes apparent that Thorkel has overheard their conversation. Thorkel's wife decides to put her arms about her husband's neck when he comes to bed that evening and to claim that the whole thing was a lie. Aud, on the other hand, says that she will tell her husband, Gisli, everything that she has left unsaid as well as all that to which she cannot find a solution (c. 9).

As the women, so the men. With Thorkel it ends up in a domestic squabble and a half-hearted reconciliation in bed, with Gisli a candid conversation ensues which concludes with almost the same words as did the misbegotten blood-brotherhood ceremony: "Whatever is meant to happen will happen" (c. 9).

Gisli bears no grudge – he has indeed no reason to. Thorkel, however, is a betrayed husband and it is understandable that Gisli is afraid of what may happen. The disclosure nevertheless provides no clarification as to why things went wrong with the blood-brotherhood ceremony as far as it concerned Thorkel and Gisli: at that time they can at most have suspected the illicit feelings that have now come to light. These may perhaps have played a part in Thorgrim's withdrawal from the ceremony. He was on the point of entering into blood-brotherhood with the man who was married to the girl he once had a relationship with. We will come back to this.

The disclosure yields no grounds for action as far as Thorkel is concerned, rather he turns it into a pretext for his secret antagonism towards Gisli to come into the open. It seems as though he is able to breathe again when he discovers his wife's betrayal. The circumstances of his overhearing the women's conversation are telling. Though they are in the midst of the busiest time of the harvest and Gisli, with whom he shares the farm and its labours, is at work day and night, Thorkel is lying in the fire room at home loafing.

The laziness is a manifestation of the purposelessness that Thorkel experiences in his inferiority to Gisli. It is an impotent act of defiance. And the noble Gisli succeeds only in exacerbating Thorkel's sense of inferiority when he lets things slide and allows Thorkel to loaf about without reproach.

But when Thorkel hears the conversation he has at last found a peg on which to hang his disgruntlement. There is an air of triumph about the verse that he utters at this climactic moment:

> Hear a great wonder
> hear of peace broken
> hear of a great matter
> hear of a death
> – one man's or more. (c. 9, II 9)

The laziness is blown away. He severs the communal living arrangement he has had with Gisli and moves to Thorgrim's neighbouring farm of Saebol. Events pick up speed.

In the brothers' youth in Norway a third situation arose which reveals the seed of the conflict between them. Bard is the name of a man who causes their sister Thordis's reputation to suffer. People say that he has seduced her and brags about it into the bargain.

Thorkel is a friend of Bard's and behaves as if nothing has happened. Gisli, thinking of his sister's honour and that of the family, kills Bard:

> Thorkel was angry and told Gisli that he had done a great wrong. Gisli told his brother to calm down and jested with him.
> "We'll swap swords," he said, "then you'll have the one with the better bite." (c. 2, II 2-3)

The weapon functions here as the signifying part of a symbolic reality, just as later in a more developed way does the weapon Grey-side, which reappears constantly throughout the course of the action. The signified part of the symbol is this: *you* as the eldest ought to have fulfilled the duty that I have now taken over.

Once again we see the two brothers facing the same challenge – the duty to restore the family's honour – and again they react differently.

In the blood-brotherhood scene two kinds of *friendship* collide. Gisli and Vestein will go through fire and water for each other, we already understand this and subsequently see their loyalty confirmed on a number of occasions. Thorkel and Thorgrim have not established the same deep friendship. Their reaction to Gisli and Vestein – that is to say, Thorkel's tacit acceptance of Thorgrim's break with the others –

can be seen in the light of what follows to be the first indication of Thorkel's spite and envy. A difference in human qualities between the two pairs of friends begins to manifest itself already at this time.

In what follows the two women's private conversation, one can read a contrast between two other kinds of human relationship, between two kinds of *marriage*. Thorkel and his wife become reconciled quickly and superficially. Between Gisli and Aud no split ever opens. On the contrary, they together turn their gaze towards the split outside them which they fear. "Whatever is meant to happen will happen."

In the scenes set in Norway we encounter an issue which is also absolutely central to the saga: two ways to conduct oneself with respect to one's *kinship:* Thorkel who takes the easy way and behaves as if there is no problem, Gisli who lives up to his duty – as he understands it – to exact blood vengeance. It is extremely telling that, once Gisli has performed it, Thorkel again chooses the comfortable way and shortly afterwards renews his friendship with Gisli, the killer of his friend. "Gisli's reputation was thought to have increased considerably as a result of this affair" (c. 2, II 4) reads the conclusion of this passage – the usual device used by the saga-writer to reveal his own judgement without stating it in so many words.

It is tempting to content oneself with this judgment, accepting the evaluation of the anonymous collective and the narrator alike. Gisli and Thorkel just happen to be men of different qualities. The origin of their tragic conflict, according to this view, lies in this discrepancy between the two and not in any specific transgression. The question arises, can we not push the analysis a step further and ask by what kind of yardstick the two men can be said to have different qualities? It is a fact of life that metals come in different degrees of fineness. But degrees of fineness are not absolutes in themselves nor a universal measure of worth. There are yardsticks appropriate to particular situations. We shall try to define those that work for *Gisli's Saga*.

But before we set to work we must demonstrate that Gisli, despite the lamentable acts he later commits, can without any doubt be described as the finer of the two.

Gisli murders his sister's husband, Thorgrim. It requires real storytelling skill to portray as noble a man who behaves in this way. It demands quite simply that he be presented as having no better choice. This is achieved with the aid of a subtle sequence of events.

The first thing that happens is that Gisli's friend Vestein is murdered. All we learn about the murderer is that he comes from Saebol, the farm where the two brothers-in-law and friends, Thorkel and Thorgrim, now live together after Gisli and Thorkel became alienated.

We are not told who the murderer is. The arrival of Vestein's murderer is described as follows: "Just before daybreak someone entered the house silently and walked over to where Vestein was lying" (c. 13, II 14). Since Thorgrim is later murdered in revenge, it is natural to think of him. The scribe of the oldest known manuscript evidently made the same connection, as the rubric he introduced above the chapter indicates. And no reader had challenged him until Anne Holtsmark (1951) read the saga and put forward the proposal that the death of Gisli's best friend was the work of Gisli's own brother, Thorkel.

Thorgrim and Thorkel share a common enmity towards Gisli and Vestein from the moment that the four friends split into two pairs during the misbegotten attempt to enter into blood-brotherhood. But the conflict comes to a head in Thorkel. He along with Gisli is foregrounded throughout the story; he is the one with the motive to kill Vestein – sexual jealousy – even if it emerges late; and he has the motive of Cain to harm his good brother, who always does the right thing. All of these serve as evidence against Thorkel. To them we may add the hint on the saga writer's part that comes near the saga's conclusion. While it is true that Thorgrim is murdered in an act intended to avenge the death of Vestein, as if he were the killer, Thorkel himself is likewise killed, in his case by Vestein's sons, who evidently regard him as a legitimate vengeance target.

An external indicator also points to Thorkel. At the division of the inheritance between the two brothers, the sword Grey-side falls to Thorkel. He and Thorgrim (with the help of a sorcerer!) have reforged it into a spear. What this detail makes clear is that Thorgrim and Thorkel have made common cause. But Grey-side is not on this account less an instrument of Thorkel's will, just as in the Bard episode the sword served the family in a similar way. Grey-side is and will always be Thorkel's inheritance.

The criminological discussion of "who killed Vestein?" was not brought to a close by Anne Holtsmark's efforts at detection. There are later scholars who have opposed her (see Andersson 1969). Nevertheless, the fact remains that Thorkel is deeply implicated in the murder, whether he carried it out with his own hands or through Thorgrim. In his turn Gisli conceals the telltale murder weapon that he finds in Vestein's body before anyone else has had a chance to see it.

So Gisli's dilemma is this: his brother-in-law and best friend have been killed and his brother is either the killer or at least his accomplice. To leave Vestein unavenged is a defeat according to the very conventions — and society — for which Gisli has been the unbending champion from the beginning of the saga. To murder his own brother is a desperate expedient. He chooses the scarcely less desperate solution of shifting the vengeance to Thorkel's co-conspirator or agent, Thorgrim. But the man he kills in this act is his sister's husband, so in spite of everything it is his own family that suffers his violence.

The rules of vengeance, which exist to protect the family, lead on the contrary to its destruction. Whatever Gisli chooses at this point will be wrong. It is against this background that he can murder a member of his own family and yet appear as a man of distinction in the saga writer's view.

The remainder of the saga, after the two murders in which it climaxes, serves to develop and support the high estimation of Gisli Sursson. This part of the saga can be read for itself as a collection of tall tales illustrating the ideal of the hero who only gives way after struggling for a long time against fifteen men and who in his last stand tries to gather his own bowels back into his belly. But the construction of the story about Gisli the outlaw reveals that its purpose is greater than simply to tell a collection of tall tales. Here the difference in quality between the two brothers that we encounter in the introduction is elaborated, which is one of the causes that things go wrong between them.

The means of accomplishing this elaboration are two: on the one hand, a continuous comparison of the two brothers, on the other, the description of Gisli's outer and inner strength.

We are informed that Gisli was the Icelander who — apart from Grettir — lived longest in outlawry (c. 22). That he was able to accomplish this is a tribute to his personal qualities and to his marriage. Whereas Thorkel, as we have seen, lives in an empty relationship with a woman who does not think much of him, Gisli loves his wife so much that he risks danger to visit her (c. 24). He knows that she esteems him so highly that he need not be afraid, even when everything indicates she is on the point of selling his life (c. 32-34). And the confidence is justified: it was only a cunning stratagem on Aud's part against Gisli's pursuers, as it turns out.

Naturally his personal attributes include the physical strength that is described in almost every one of the episodes that constitute his outlawry; there is also the ingenuity to which he has recourse when the strength of his enemies is too great. In both these respects he exceeds not merely his elder brother, but all the men he comes up against. In addition his personal qualities include a spiritual strength that expresses itself through the dreams he has and his interpretation of them. Gisli is a "truth-dreamer," who knows himself and does not attempt to put a brave face on his situation. What we shall now attempt to determine is the yardstick according to which Gisli is judged a better man than Thorkel.

Gisli gives himself away in a confrontation with his sister Thordis (c. 18). He does so in a verse, but the hint does not escape Thordis. Gisli, conversely, has trouble understanding her reaction. She incites her new husband and former brother-in-law Bork to take revenge on Gisli. "I don't think I deserved this from her," says Gisli when he hears what his sister has set in train against him (c. 19, II 23). In view of the occasion – Gisli has murdered his sister's husband – one would not expect him to be so surprised. Meanwhile he compares her reaction in this case to another of his actions in relation to her:

> "I thought I made it clear several times that her honour meant no less to me than my own. There were even times when I put my life in danger for her sake, and now she has pronounced my death sentence." (c. 19, II 23)

What Gisli is referring to is his behaviour during their younger years together in Norway, the time when he killed one of her suitors, crippled a second, and brought to an end her relationship with a third. He is puzzled that she is not so grateful for these acts that she would refrain from vengeance now, when for different reasons he has undertaken a comparable course of action for the fourth time: namely killed her husband. It does not occur to Gisli that Thordis has not forgotten her previous gratefulness – she never felt it.

"There was rumour abroad that Bard had seduced Thordis" (c. 2, II 2). Her father does not approve of this. Thorkel is indifferent to his father's disapproval and maintains his friendship with Bard. Gisli, on the other hand, acts in accordance with his father's wishes and kills Bard.

Skeggi the Dueller proposes to Thordis. Her father disapproves of the match. After various intrigues, Gisli fights a duel with him and cuts off his leg.

The intrigues are set in motion by yet another man, Kolbjorn, who is said to be having an affair with Thordis. He would gladly take up Skeggi's challenge in return for the promise that he himself can have Thordis. Gisli refuses in behalf of his family. With this Kolbjorn declines to face Skeggi, which reveals his cravenness and renders his suit impossible.

In all three cases the saga informs us of the father's wishes and also of Gisli's, which correspond closely to them. Gisli translates the family's desires into action. In none of the three occasions does the saga inform us of Thordis's desires. The rumours about the affairs in which she has been engaged might of course be mistaken. But if the appearance of smoke does not infallibly prove the existence of a fire, so much smoke without fire stretches probability. The saga's silence about Thordis's desires compared with its insistence on the recurrent rumours about these desires can scarcely be understood unless as evidence that she *does have* desires – and that they part company with her father's. And from Gisli's which are identical with his father's.

The collision in the preparatory conflicts is one between two conceptions of the current rules for the display of passion. Thordis does nothing to counteract the negative interpretations sanctioned by the unflattering rumours, even if it is in her power to do so. When the situation is repeated, she continues to do nothing to silence them. It is her passivity in regard to the rules or more probably – since her behaviour is repeated – her actions *against* the rules, that bring about the first open breech between Gisli and Thorkel: Gisli kills Thorkel's friend.

The fourth man to court Thordis is Thorgrim, the man whom Gisli will come to murder. And the fifth, Thordis's second husband, is the person who arranges the killing of Gisli. Had Thordis not been an attractive woman, and had she not – in defiance of her father's wishes – before her marriage broken the rules of how such things should be done, the first quarrel between Gisli and Thorkel could have been avoided. Thordis's men enter as instruments in all the destruction that the saga tells of. And she attracts men whose compulsions cause them to set conventions aside: Bard, Skeggi – and Thorgrim, who breaks up the blood-brotherhood ceremony after he had freely agreed to participate in it. Does it play a role in the current transaction, which cannot be explained rationally considering that it comes as a surprise, that the men he is swearing blood-brotherhood with are the brother and husband of the woman, Aud, with whom he *no longer* has a relationship? Thorgrim's compulsiveness is at the very least thrown into relief by the way in which his relationship with Thordis comes about.

> Thorgrim, the son of Thorstein, found Thordis, the sister of Gisli and Thorkel, very attractive and asked for her hand in marriage. She was betrothed to him and the wedding followed soon in the wake of the betrothal. (c. 5, II 6)

It is clear, on the basis of the proposal and the pace at which the wedding comes about, that desire takes precedence over concern for dowry and family arrangements, even if in this instance the two do not come into conflict, for Thorgrim is a man of considerable influence who is valuable to have as an in-law. Still, the normal order of events – first family approval, then proposal and wedding – is reversed. The reversal may well be a sign indicating that conventions are called into doubt or at all events not adhered to chapter and verse. It is in Thordis's proximity that this doubt occurs, in connection with her own evolving desires. One almost never sees her acting in her own name, until indeed she makes the symbolic attempt to stab Gisli's murderer between his legs with a sword: an impotent protest against the action she has herself set in motion behind the scenes. That is where her most important role is played. She exists as the essence of sexuality off-stage, her counterpart on stage is Thorkel. He assumes the same problematic relationship to the rigid social conventions as she does and like her he finds himself playing out his part with Gisli as his antagonist.

We have already spoken of how Thorkel decides to proceed in the face of Gisli's first action in conformity with ancestral convention – the killing of his sister's lover and Thorkel's friend: he comes to terms first with his friend's destructive impact on his sister's reputation, then with Gisli's murder of his friend.

At the other end of the story he behaves in accordance with the same imperatives. When Bork has let himself be incited by Thordis Thorkel at first tries to dissuade him from his plans:

> "On the other hand, I can't be sure," [Thorkel] said, "how much truth there is in what Thordis says. It's just as likely that there's none. Women's counsel is often cold." (c. 19, II 23)

When this trivialising effort seems not to have succeeded, he secretly seeks out Gisli and warns him against Bork. It is at this point that Gisli utters the previously cited answer: that he cannot understand how Thordis can have forgotten the sense of gratitude he thinks she must feel towards him for having saved her reputation on a number of occasions in Norway!

It is a tribute to the saga that in conflicts such as this, despite the sympathetic light cast on Gisli, the detached observer is enabled to see Gisli's limitations. He lives and thinks within a set of conventions that reveal themselves to be incapable of containing and guiding the urges that actually drive human behaviour.

Gisli asks his brother for help and secures an answer he himself would never have given:

> "I can give you warning if there is an attempt on your life," said Thorkel, "but I can afford you no help that might lead to my being accused." (c. 19, II 23)

To Gisli's either-or mentality this is incomprehensible. He repeats the request on three later occasions (c. 21, 23, 24) with the same – from his point of view – incomprehensible result.

Later he finds himself in a situation that parallels Thorkel's. The sons of murdered Vestein kill Thorkel. It is the fulfilment of the vengeance that Gisli himself initiated with the murder of Thorgrim. But Thorkel happens to be Gisli's brother and he is unwilling even to see his brother's murderers. He jumps up and grabs his sword when he hears from Aud that the two lads – his nephews! – have arrived after the killing. Fortunately they have already departed again and Gisli's ill-fortuned, mechanical consistency is not required to go that monstrous step further.

For Gisli there is no way back into society. The step he so nearly took in relation to Vestein's sons has only carried him further away from that. The one thing left to sustain him is the growing inner strength of his relationship with Aud and of his relation with himself. In these respects his stature reaches immense proportions.

Had he taken Thorkel's path, he might have been able to avoid some of the killings, perhaps all of them. Whether in doing so he could be said to have avoided "the worst" depends on our judgment of the conflicting conventions available to guide his actions. Following the convention that he adopts, and that the saga writer through his admiration of Gisli endorses – the family-centred rules – he has no choice. According to this view, the worst response is Thorkel's half-measures. In view of the pragmatic conventions which are exemplified by the behaviour of Thorkel and Thordis at the beginning of the saga, however, he did have a choice.

What we witness in *Gisli's Saga* is a collision between two kinds of morality, an old and a new one. The saga writer aligns himself with the old values but *at the same time*, his story shows how they come up short because they do not accommodate all the motivations on which humans act. These include jealousy between brothers and the imperative of achievement which, when they arise within the same family, have destructive effects. And further in the background we find erotic impulse as the second pattern.

The first conflict, the killing of the sister's illicit lover, arises in the interplay between the two patterns. The remainder of the conflicts are found in germ here.

Prior to the Norwegian pre-history, in the generation before, the same war of impulses plays itself out in outline form, but with a different outcome (c. 1). Here the old convention still governs so firmly that it can heal the breach and hold the family together.

Gisli's uncle Ari is sought out by a berserk – and berserks are people who break the peace. Bjorn, the berserk in question, wants Ari's wife, so he gives Ari two choices: either he will say yes or he must engage in a duel. Naturally he chooses the duel, but falls.

At that point the family-centred rules come into play. Gisli's other uncle, also called Gisli, takes his place by the widow's side to answer the thieving berserk. As a foreshadowing of later events this is the man she would in fact have preferred to marry. With the help of a sword that he borrows from the widow's thrall, this earlier Gisli succeeds in re-establishing order: he eliminates the berserk and marries the widow.

This does not tie up all loose ends, though. The instrument of retribution, the sword, remains; the thrall wants it back, but Gisli the elder is unwilling to part with it. Both die in their fight for it.

So the initial struggle brings about the death of no less than four men. That much it takes to have the family cleansed, both of the interloper and of the man who participated in the illicit sexual attachment within the family. Among the survivors are Gisli Sursson's father and the sword, which stays in the family. The sword is Greyside.

Thus it is that the old convention functions for the last time as it was intended to. When it comes into play against the irregularities of the next generation, it leads to the destruction of the family.

Gisli's Saga, which is not merely one of the most successful, perfectly achieved and nuanced art works among sagas of Icelanders, but also one of the most secretive yet coherent articulations of the second pattern, is at the same time a good occasion to warn against a possible misinterpretation of the nature of this pattern.

We who are separated from the sagas by the nineteenth century can easily be misled into believing that the overriding moral calamity is that of Victorian morality: sexual intercourse. It is not.

Thordis may or may not have had sexual relations with her alleged lovers, and Aud with Thorgrim. That is not the heart of the matter. What is certain — what distinguishes these women, as it also distinguishes Aud from Thorkel's wife — is that Aud can say that she has never had a relationship "that caused harm to any one," that is to say she has not acted behind Gisli's back.

Thordis damages her family's reputation, which threatens the family's unity comprising legal marriages and possessions, *and she does nothing to repair this damage*. Asgerd's heart is set upon Vestein and she does not care if her husband knows it.

The decisive issue is whether the urge that transgresses legal and family-approved bonds between people is tamed and socialized or whether it is acted out regardless of the social consequences. The profound division between *one* of the various actions in which it can appear and all the others, the saga does not know. The saga's second pattern deals with erotic impulse, not with the subsection known as the sexual act. That distinction can only be read into *Kormak's Saga*, which may certainly make us suspect that we are being influenced by the nineteenth century when we do so.

CHAPTER 4

THE ICELANDIC MYTH

Njal's Saga

Of all the sagas of Icelanders, the one about Njal has remained the most popular over the years, judging by extant versions and readers' assessments.

No other saga is preserved in so many manuscripts, a score of more or less incomplete texts from before 1550, twice as many since. And scarcely any other has been so frequently translated or edited. In Danish alone at least eight translators have attempted it. The number of editions is double this. Icelandic scholars often refer to the saga's great popularity in every age. "And in the present it is no less esteemed," writes Finnur Jónsson in his literary history of 1898. "The present author knew a child who had read the saga ten times by the time he was ten years old." Presumably the child was named Finnur.

One may wonder why *Njal's Saga* has outshone the other sagas to the extent indicated by these measures.

This unique popularity cannot be accounted for simply by the saga's artistic qualities. The explanation, in my opinion, must be sought in the quality for which Finnur Jónsson admires it: no other saga is so rich a source of Iceland's history, no matter how reliable a source it is. In *Kormak's Saga* we find information about the rules of dueling, in *Gisli's Saga* rules about entering into blood-brotherhood and so on. No other saga contains as much and as important information of this kind as *Njal's Saga*. The introduction of Christianity into Iceland and Icelandic court procedures are described in *Njal's Saga* with a thoroughness and detail not found in any other saga of Icelanders. The country emerges as never before. It is not difficult to understand why it has become a national treasure for Icelanders.

The Danish poet and scholar Carsten Hauch, in the middle of the nineteenth century, was the first to risk judging this saga to be fiction.

Had the opinion prevailed, it would be harder to understand the extraordinary popularity of *Njal's Saga* as evidenced by the number of editions, *vis-à-vis* such sagas as *Gisli's Saga, Egil's Saga,* or *Hrafnkel's Saga*. It is difficult to take it in as a unified whole, exuberantly rich as it is in sub-plots, not to mention the occasional clumsiness. New characters, important to the narrative, appear just before they are required to play their parts, though forgotten until then and dismissed immediately afterwards. If such peculiarities have passed into the general consciousness as characteristic of sagas of Icelanders, it is because of *Njal's Saga* with its great popularity. In other equally good sagas such features are far less prominent.

But even when *Njal's Saga* is re-evaluated according to its proper merits, simply as one among many other good sagas of Icelanders, which can measure themselves against it in various ways, it remains a grand and impressive construction for the reader who penetrates its motley exterior. Its size necessitates that this chapter, even more than the preceding ones, must set aside any hope of presenting a complete analysis. Instead it will chiefly address three questions: how does what I have referred to in my first chapter as the "second pattern" reveal itself? How does the saga describe the shift from the old convention to the new, a process whose delineation shaped much of the analysis above; and finally how does the saga contribute to what I have called (in the chapter on *Laxdœla Saga*) the Icelandic myth.

Njal's Saga which has more of almost everything than any other saga, also has more misguided marriages, forced marriages, hasty marriages, and broken marriages than any of the others.

In its opening there is talk of almost nothing but such marriages. And the connection between the saga's two parts depends on – among other things – this theme. The first part culminates in the death of Gunnar of Hlidarendi. This would not have come about had it not been for two persons, Hallgerd and Mord, who are the representatives and the results of the thoughtless and asocial playing out of urges. The climax of the second part is the death of Njal and his family, the consequence of conflicts involving two people with the same characteristics, Hrapp and Thrain. Hrapp is linked to Hallgerd before she disappears from the saga, and Mord takes on the vengeance for Thrain. The saga's two parts are linked together with the help of several villains who, in addition to their villainy, share the common characteristic that they are linked together by urges that do not enjoy the blessing of society.

It might be useful, before a detailed consideration of all this, to sketch the train of events in the story:

> Already in the first scene we notice Hallgerd's beautiful hair, which will later tempt Gunnar so that he overlooks her thief's eyes. Hrut's voyage to Norway and his affair with Gunnhild lead to the dissolution of his marriage with Unn and to a conflict between him and Mord Fiddle. Gunnar succeeds, assisted by Njal's advice, in recovering Unn's dowry. When Unn once more becomes a prosperous woman, she is able to marry Valgard the Grey and the fruit of this marriage is Mord, who does not stop until Gunnar and Hoskuld Hvitanes Priest are killed and Njal and his sons have been burned in. Gunnar marries Hallgerd, daughter of his old adversary Hoskuld, Hrut's brother, and his life as a hero, which he did not want, begins. Njal's wife, Bergthora, and Hallgerd start bickering and strain the friendship between Gunnar and Njal. Hallgerd steals and brings Gunnar into disrepute. Despite Njal's assistance and good advice, this ends with Gunnar's stalwart self-defence and death. There follows a struggle between Njal's sons and Thrain Sigfusson, Gunnar's uncle and Hallgerd's son-in-law, whom Skarphedin kills. Njal acts bravely; he defies the requirement of father-vengeance, which is otherwise described, in the story of blind Amundi, as pleasing to God – a view which must cause the bewildered reader to ponder; he adopts Hoskuld Thrainsson and lets him grow up among the murderers of his father. A man of peace and law, he plays a dangerous game to stop the cycle of vengeance and loss, when his sons and Kari – led astray by Mord Valgardsson – thwart his endeavours by killing Hoskuld, thus helping Mord Valgardsson to even the score with the man who had robbed him of his priestly status. His wife, whom Njal on dubious moral grounds had obtained for Hoskuld, demands vengeance and gets her uncle Flosi involved. Bergthorshvol burns. Njal comes to terms with his fate and Skarphedin atones for his offence. There follows a great lawsuit which demonstrates the powerlessness of law and right, Kari's cleansing expedition of vengeance and the final reconciliation, which depends upon the power of a merciful God to whom Njal had previously bowed and whom Flosi and Kari too with their pilgrimages recognise as stronger than a sinful human's upright will. Kari marries Flosi's niece, who has been widowed by the man she marries.

The first dangerous woman, Hallgerd, is introduced in Chapter 1 and the first risky engagement, between Hrut and Unn, occurs in Chapter 2. It happens at the prompting of Hoskuld, a brave man who anticipates Njal's role in his giving of well-intentioned advice, concerning both this and the following marriage, each of which proves to be ill-advised. The uselessness of well-intentioned advice is a recurrent motif in the saga.

The reason that everything goes wrong between Hrut and Unn is that shortly before the marriage, Hrut sails for Norway to collect an unexpected inheritance and, as mentioned in the summary, becomes Queen Gunhild's lover. The saga writer uses magic to explain what comes of this relationship. When Hrut takes his leave of Gunhild, she lays a curse on him that he will henceforward not be able to have sexual relations with the woman he loves, though with others he will be unimpaired. One does not have to be a magician to find the result believable. Potency in illicit relationships and impotence in the licit one has been observed and described by other than magicians. If psychoanalysts had known this story, they could have used it as a textbook example of one of the theories of impotence. The marriage is celebrated at home in Iceland without joy. And since it is never consummated, Unn can use her right to declare herself divorced.

The description of Unn's next marriage includes an important detail: "she married Valgard without the advice of his kinsmen" (c. 25, III 30). As someone formerly married she had the right to do so, according to the statute supposedly in effect in Iceland then, a law – as it happens – first imported from Norway in 1272 and not the old Icelandic statute that would have been in force at the time of the story. But neither statute is crucial here. As we shall see, *Njal's Saga* is, among other things, an account of how the rule of statutes fails.

What is decisive is that marriage and kinship no longer constitute the unbreakable unity that a society such as that in Iceland presupposes. Unn follows her own direction and introduces into the family "a mean spirited and unpopular man" (c. 25, III 30). And the result of the union, their son Mord, grows into a man who was "bad to his kinsmen, and to Gunnar worst of all. He was devious by nature and malicious in his counsels" (c. 25, III 30).

This may seem a meager motivation for Mord's villainous role, but the saga provides no other. Either we accept as a pure given that this schemer-in-chief is a schemer by nature, or we have to seize on his engendering, as heir to a man with the same predilections. It is a woman's wilfulness and disregard for her family that has caused these predilections to be introduced into it.

The other dangerous woman in the prelude, Hallgerd, is not thus motivated. From the beginning it is a puzzle how her thief's eyes have come into the family. On the other hand, we get to know so much more about what comes of them.

Her marriages too, all three of them, are questionable in terms of family law and morals. The first, like Unn's first, is a purely economic arrangement between suitor and family. Indeed it is stressed that Hallgerd is not even consulted. When she hears about the arrangement, she is opposed to it. This combination – an enthusiastic family and an unenthusiastic bride – is problematic and has fatal consequences. Already at the wedding (c. 10) she begins to plot with her foster-father Thjostolf. She provokes the husband imposed upon her and receives a slap on the face, after which Thjostolf kills him. Hallgerd's father is Hoskuld. So this is the second time he gets into trouble arranging the affairs of others.

By the third time, he has become wiser. When Glum comes courting his now widowed daughter, he avoids speaking on her behalf. But Hallgerd, when consulted, accepts his suit. She is married to Glum and the happiness of their life together is repeatedly stressed.

Nevertheless, a shadow follows from Hallgerd's first, unlucky marriage, her foster-father Thjostolf. The people surrounding them have been aware of the danger and advised the couple to stipulate that Thjostolf may not live with them unless both spouses wish it. Hallgerd begs Glum to give his permission, and because they are happy together he can see no reason to deny her the pleasure. Thjostolf succeeds in sewing division between them, to the point that Glum slaps Hallgerd – which does not, however, destroy her love for him. The scheme fails. Thjostolf must therefore kill Glum on his own initiative, after first having reproached him for having "no strength for anything except bouncing around on Hallgerd's belly" (c. 17, III 22). In other words the death takes place against the background of an explicit reference to sexuality. The evil forces that Hallgerd allies herself with during her first, forced marriage intervene destructively in her second freely-chosen and sexually fulfilling marriage.

Such is Hallgerd's life story until the moment she meets Gunnar at a thing and a powerful urge draws them together. Her father and uncle advise against the union out of respect for Gunnar, but without any luck. They get married and things proceed very much as they had during Hallgerd's first two marriages: provocations by Hallgerd, much more numerous than before and repeatedly deflected by Gunnar and his friend, the peace-maker Njal; finally a slap and at last, long after the slap, Hallgerd lets down Gunnar in retaliation at a moment where she could have saved him from death.

During the wedding feast itself a remarkable situation develops. Among the guests are the bridegroom's uncle Thrain and the bride's daughter, by her second marriage, Thorgerd. The aged man is smitten by the fourteen-year old girl, on the spot he declares himself divorced from his wife – who is also present at the wedding! – and is immediately married to Thorgerd (c. 34).

The next time this hot-tempered man turns up is at Hallgerd's side during the execution of the fifth of the deaths by which she and Njal's wife alternately attempt to incite their husbands against each other (c. 41). We see him in a similar role in the central action, when Gunnar is killed and the main conflict shifts to Njal's family. Thrain is a participant in this process.

It is in Norway that the animosity between him and the sons of Njal originates. A trouble-maker named Hrapp is sheltered by Thrain during the former's flight, but the sons of Njal are blamed for this by their common host, Earl Hakon. This is the first step in their path to enmity. The rescued Hrapp turns up in Iceland for the first time in flight from the supporters of the man he has murdered. In Norway he abducts a farmer's daughter and desecrates a shrine (c. 87). At home in Iceland he settles down with Thrain and Hallgerd and begins making advances to Gudrun; some said that he was seducing her. This is the man who plays a large part in the later developments that lead to the Njalssons' killing of Thrain. And when that deed is accomplished, the train of events is set in motion that will end in the burning-in at Bergthorshvol. The groundwork is laid for the project that Mord Valgardsson will bring to a conclusion.

In sum, we have four villains: Hallgerd, Mord, Hrapp and Thrain. Eliminate them and there would be no story. What unites them, apart from the abstract quality of malignity (which manifests itself variously but palpably) is that all four are in different ways engendered by or entangled in erotic behaviour that runs counter to the social norm.

This pattern is not the whole story. But it is an important constituent of the opening stages of each of the sequences of events that comprise the saga. It comes up so frequently that it forms a pattern. The erotic disorder and the social disorder appear to be two sides of the same coin.

Until now, our discussion has been preoccupied with the origins of things. Let us now turn from the forces that set events in motion to the forces that delay or resist the rise of the conflict and let us focus on the course of the conflicts and question the role played in them by the law and by peace-makers. It will turn out to be problematic.

In his analysis, Hauch wanted to trace Njal's complicity back to the sin of which he is guilty very early in the saga when he prompts Gunnar to commit a piece of fraud. It is when Unn has left her ill-fortuned marriage with Hrut and seeks her kinsman Gunnar's help in recovering her dowry. The problem is how to serve a summons on Hrut. Njal advises Gunnar to disguise himself as a hawker and in this way to engage Hrut in conversation. Njal, the lawyer, in this way makes use of a trick which will later be avenged ten-fold.

More striking than this "sin," however, is the way in which Njal's entirely well-intentioned and perfectly legal procedures, which ought to further peace and stability, contrary to their purpose advance the conflicts and disrupt the communities.

It has often been pointed out by scholars from Denmark (Hauch), Sweden (Bååth), and Iceland (Sveinsson) how Njal's advice never works, not only the advice about Unn's money but also about Thrain's marriage with Thorgerd. I have attempted to show how Hoskuld in this respect is a parallel-figure to Njal. On top of such unintended mischiefs even the actions Njal undertakes with the express intention of containing the ill-luck promote it.

Njal's prophecy that things will go badly for Gunnar, if he kills twice in the same family, can be understood not only as a prophecy about what will happen, but also as a common-sense warning not to stir up too much enmity in one family. This is simply what sound judgment dictates. But expressed as a prophecy it achieves the opposite effect: the prophecy becomes known to Gunnar's opponents and is used by them to lay legal traps so that Gunnar inadvertently lands in the specified situation (c. 72).

The most dangerous strategy that Njal embarks on, as mentioned in my initial summary of the plot, is his transaction with Hoskuld Thrainsson. And it is not just that his sons thwart his strategy; the ominous consequences are part and parcel of Njal's very strategy.

Njal adopts Thrain's son, whose father his sons have murdered. And in order to make the reconciliation complete, he arranges that Hoskuld shall have a wife of rank who is also Hoskuld's own choice, Hildigunn.

Njal has some difficulty in establishing the connection, but he does not ease off until he has succeeded. The difficulties arise from Hildigunn's unwillingness to marry Hoskuld unless he has a godord, that is, a chieftaincy. Njal sets about obtaining one for him. But from this good intention two evil consequences derive.

The obtaining of a godord for Hoskuld – in a completely legal way – means a reduction in the power of other godi or chieftains. One of them is the wicked Mord, who thus gains a motive to turn his malice against Njal and to stir up bad blood between the Njalssons and Hoskuld. This happens with the help of a swindle for which Njal – although he is not a participant – has prepared the ground, despite the nobility of his intentions.

The other consequence of Hoskuld's marriage into a strong family is that Njal by suggesting the marriage creates his own slayer. By allying Hoskuld with a man of Flosi's strength Njal intended to reconcile Hoskuld and thus secure the peace. However, had this alliance not been created – under Njal's influence – there would have been no Flosi among those who burned Njal in vengeance for Hoskuld's death.

We may conclude: it is precisely Njal's efforts at conciliation that keep the conflict going once it has begun. His good will leads to evil. The ties of kinship are created in order to avoid the conflict. But they only manage to make the kin-enmity even deadlier. A bloodier conflict than that which follows the fire at Bergthorshvol is not to be found in the sagas of Icelanders.

Njal's attempt to prevent the blood-letting with the help of the law is also worth studying. "With laws shall our land be built up," he comments, citing a proverb known throughout medieval Scandinavia, that expresses the sense of a community based on laws. But consider what he does.

Njal is a great lawyer. Thorhall Asgrimsson, whom Njal trains, gains so extensive a knowledge of law that he becomes "one of the three greatest lawyers in Iceland" (c. 109, III 132). It is by means of his insight into the law that Njal is able to establish the godord for Hoskuld that he needs for his reconciliation plan.

It will not do simply to ask the other godar if they would be so kind as to give up a little of their power to accommodate Njal's foster-son. Iceland is fully settled. What is to be given to one must be taken from another – this is an important factor in the stage of societal evolution portrayed by the sagas, as we shall see below. Njal understands this and the need to achieve his goal by means of the Socratic method, which has always been a good device for masking the work of authority.

> Njal tried to find a godord for Hoskuld, but no one was willing to sell his.
> The summer moved on until time for the Althing. That year there were many lawsuits, and as usual many people came to consult Njal, but he gave advice which, unlikely as it seemed, ruined both prosecution and defense and led to much wrangling when cases could not be settled, and men rode home from the Thing unreconciled. (c. 97, III 116)

Njal has a purpose in mind with this special legal assistance. He wants to show people that the institutions of justice are incomplete, since a court of higher instance is lacking beyond the four Quarter Courts for cases which have clearly become stalled and for which no recourse is available. People need a fifth court, a kind of appeal court.

> The wisest course, in my opinion, would be to have a Fifth Court and prosecute cases there that can't be settled in the Quarter Courts. (c. 97, III 116)

But how should this Fifth Court be composed? Njal, to be sure, has a plan. Outstanding men in each Quarter should be named as new godar and those inhabitants who want to should be allowed to transfer their allegiance to these new chieftains, who will in turn constitute the new Fifth Court. One needs to bear in mind in this connection that the word godord designated neither a region nor a parish or county, but rather an authority whose strength depended on the loyalty of followers who were at any time free to withdraw their allegiance from one chieftain and transfer it to another.

In other words, Njal first engineers a dilemma which is obvious to everyone: the lack of a superior court. Then he proposes a solution for the dilemma which gives him as a bonus the chance to obtain the extra chieftaincy he needs for his foster-son.

The Romantic scholar N.M. Petersen, who regarded the saga as an historical account of the real life of Icelanders, considered this move on Njal's part one of his contributions to his country. Prior to the introduction of the Fifth Court difficult cases were either stalled or resolved by a duel: "from this time Icelandic legal procedures, after Njal's wise advice, had reached their completion" (2nd ed. 1862, II 183f).

The story that the saga tells is somewhat different, to say the least. Dueling was discontinued, in Petersen's view, because it was supposed to have been made obsolete as a means of legal redress as a result of Njal's innovation. Yet in the saga the first action brought after the institution of the Fifth Court, the case against those who burned Njal in, ends not simply in a single duel between two men, but in a fierce battle at the Althing itself. There is something awry in this assessment of the wise Njal's judicial contribution.

The problem is that what N.M. Petersen calls the completion of the legal institution, the saga-writer in his narrative employs to demonstrate its imperfection. Apparently, with laws our land cannot be built up.

Regrettably it is the custom of editors, when they abbreviate *Njal's Saga*, to make their largest cuts in the legal hairsplitting in the saga's final third, since they find them too tiresome. But in their own way the legal quibbles are more important to the overall structure of the saga than are the many repetitions the editors carefully retain, for example, the murders executed alternately by the two women at Bergthorshvol and Hlidarendi as they attempt to destroy their husbands' friendship. These are repeated six times without adding anything new. For the meaning is not that death is unimportant.

Something of this sort, on the other hand, is the implication of the endless repetitions in the conclusion of the formal charges against the man who has given Njal's son Helgi "a brain wound or internal wound or marrow wound." As Martin Larsen shows, this is a somewhat unthinking citation from a law code rather than a case of documentary realism: the irrelevant alternatives of the multiple choice should have been struck out. But as the saga shows, the implication of the repetition is the pointlessness of formalism, for each time the charge is repeated, a new judicial technicality arises which means that it must later be heard once again.

The most important of these complications is a direct consequence of Njal's reforms.

Flosi has a hard time clearing himself. The clever Eyjolf then provides assistance. Njal had determined which actions should be referred to the Fifth Court. Among these are cases pleaded before the wrong court. This gives Eyjolf an idea:

> You must give up your godord and place it in the hands of your brother Thorgeir, and then declare yourself a thingman of Askel Thorketilsson the Godi, from up north in Reykjadal. If they don't find out about this it may do them some damage: they will bring their suit in the East Quarter Court when – although they will not be aware of this – they should bring it in the North Quarter Court. Then they will be liable to an action in the Fifth Court for bringing a suit in the wrong court. (c. 141, III 179)

Interest is diverted from the facts of the case to its formalities, whose nooks and crannies men can use to their own advantage, if they are sufficient hair-splitters. The law is no longer the means by which the land will be built, but rather an institution that keeps wounds open and delays their healing. Njal's judicial initiatives related to the reconciliation after Thrain's death provide the precondition for this degeneration of the law. Without his death there would have been no Fifth Court.

What we witness in *Njal's Saga* is not so much a judicial sin followed by atonement (Hauch's view) as a demonstration of the paradox that the growth of legal institutions equals the decay of the rule of law.

When a settlement is at the point of being arranged after the killing of Hoskuld – much money has been contributed – Njal lays a costly silk cloak on top of the assembled valuables in order to demonstrate his good will. It is precisely this act that leads to the breaking of the settlement at the last moment (c. 123).

Throughout the narrative, from Njal's advice in the beginning to Gunnar that he disguise himself as Hawker-Hedin to regain Unn's money, to Njal's final advice to the chieftains proposing the creation of a Fifth Court so that Hoskuld can obtain a godord, we witness Njal – a good man with the highest respect for the law – acting to achieve peace but in actual fact causing strife. One lawyer after another wears himself out pleading his case at the Althing after the burning, but nothing comes of it.

The triumph of formalism is underscored by the singular fact that the person who voices the oft-repeated complaint on behalf of the Njalssons is none other than Mord. He has been forced to take up their case, although he was an accomplice in the destruction of Njal and his family. Yet he plays his part skilfully. The law has become a self-perpetuating mechanism serving its own interests rather than those of the victims of the real disputes it was created to manage.

Legal institutions are thriving, the rule of law is in decay.

In the midst of this fundamental shift from a time when the law was expected to solve all disputes to a time when it clearly can no longer do this, Christianity is introduced into Iceland.

This material fills a number of chapters, that like the chapters on legal material tend to suffer heavy cuts at the hands of later editors of the saga. This too is a pity, for it serves more than simply to round out the historical picture. The saga could not have been brought to a conclusion had this transition from one mental state to the next not taken place.

Njal is among the first Icelanders to embrace the new faith. It arrives late in the saga and cannot decisively change the events that are the tragic consequence of the collapse of the old order governed by the law. But it can give him comfort as he perishes in the flames of the burners.

> "Have faith that God is merciful, and that he will not let us burn both in this world and in the next." (c. 129, III 155).

This famous line of Njal's can be read not only psychologically, as an expression of Njal's stoic or Christian calm in the face of the appalling, but also structurally as a summary of the human development the entire saga tells of: the old world must be leveled so that the new one can arise. The old world is the world of the law, the new one is that of Christianity.

The battle at the Althing, which thwarted the attempt at a legal settlement for the burning in, is brought to an end. A settlement is achieved and to a large extent honoured. But peace cannot be fully re-established by means of the instruments of the old order. The killings continue. The final reconciliation becomes possible only under the rule of Christian mercy.

The two chief antagonists after the burning are Njal's surviving son-in-law, Kari, and the head of Hoskuld's widow's family, Flosi. Kari sets off at last, after many vengeance killings, on a pilgrimage to Rome and obtains forgiveness for his sins. Flosi does the same. And so at length they are able to meet on terms that the Icelandic law did not have the power to shape and in a style that the old Icelandic convention did not warrant:

> Flosi was in the main room. He recognised Kari at once and jumped up to meet him and kissed him, and then placed him in the high seat by his side. He invited Kari to stay there for the winter, and Kari accepted.
> They made a full reconciliation. Flosi then gave to Kari in marriage his brother's daughter, Hildigunn, who had been the wife of Hoskuld the Godi of Hvitanes. (c. 159, III 219)

These lines are as important to the saga's underlying myth as is the rest of the story. This evangelical scene ends the story of Gunnar and Njal and the fire at Bergthorshvol. What the old world was unable to heal, the new world could, is the lesson that this ending teaches.

Scholars who study the sagas comparatively are agreed that the author of *Njal's Saga* must have been familiar with *Laxdœla Saga*. For this reason too, *Laxdœla Saga* is a good foil against which to hold *Njal's Saga*. The mythical cycle from an original period of purity, dignity, and greatness, through a fall which is the saga's main subject, to the restoration of a new order, receives its definitive treatment in the saga about the people of Laxardal. That portion of the sequence that *Njal's Saga* depicts corresponds exactly to this pattern.

Njal's Saga omits the early period. Hallgerd's thief's eyes are noted already in the first chapter, and from this point the peace is constantly broken. But if *Njal's Saga* is short on pre-history, it does offer a powerful image of the collapse; and it presents a bitter and more thorough portrait than any other Icelandic saga of the inadequacy of a social institution such as the law, which proves incapable of keeping chaos at bay.

The coming of Christianity threatens to make what is evil worse. It is difficult enough to enforce one law, but two laws – one Icelandic, and one Christian – side by side are yet more problematic. The wise Thorgeir sees this when the situation is about to develop: "if the law is split then peace will be split, and we can't live with that." (c. 105, III 127). His countrymen agree with him and all officially accept Christianity as the basis for the country's future law. With this decision the worst is avoided and the ground is prepared upon which Kari and Flosi can finally embrace.

However entertaining *Njal's Saga* may be, it is nevertheless – like the other sagas of Icelanders – far from being mere entertainment. It is a grand narrative in which everything has a place. The law, constructed by human beings, proves unfit to govern human urges; chaos ensues and is replaced by a new order only when a new Christian foundation has been laid.

We shall soon turn to the conditions in real life that prompted this – by now familiar – mythical interpretation. But let us first take a close look at a couple of sagas from the final period of saga composition.

CHAPTER 5

POST-CLASSICAL SAGAS

Hrafnkel's Saga

If the frequent recurrences of the second pattern in the sagas begin to feel oppressive, it will be relief to turn to a saga where no ingenious searching can possibly find it, for the simple reason that the saga's characters – with the single exception of a thrall woman – are all of the same sex.

Hrafnkel's Saga is a saga about men. It is a saga about power and the relationship between power and person. And it is finally a saga which adds a new chapter to the Icelandic myth delineated in the foregoing readings.

Many readers of *Hrafnkel's Saga* have agreed that it is a moral tale, but the agreement is a good deal less general when it comes to deciding what that moral is. Either they remain silent as to the kind of moral (Andersson), or they see it as Christian (Pálsson). Both responses, as I shall try to argue, are problematic. But let us begin by looking at the story.

As in *Njal's Saga* and *Gisli's Saga* things go badly for the title character, but unlike Njal and Gisli, Hrafnkel is not killed. And the saga does not end with his downfall. Rather the story picks up again and, unlike the just-mentioned sagas, ends with the hero having gained twice what he had earlier lost. He loses power as chieftain in Hrafnkelsdal; he moves to Fljotsdal where he establishes a new power comparable to what he had lost; and the saga ends with him in possession of both authorities.

Unlike other sagas about the loss of power and its re-establishment on a new foundation, this is a story of the concentration of power. It is read by some as the story of a change of heart. And it is true that we see now one, now another character in Hrafnkel. But what such a reading ignores is that both Hrafnkel's characters serve one and the same purpose. If his character changes, it is because his circumstances require it; and when his circumstances change once again to his advantage, the cause – among other things – is that he has been able to assume the character best suited to gaining his ends. It is not a saga about penance and recovery; rather it is a saga about expediency and how to recover power.

This interpretation requires documentation for it runs counter to the established reading of *Hrafnkel's Saga*.

One autumn Hrafnkel hires a poor man's son, Einar, as a shepherd, he sets him the same rules as his other servants regarding the handling of his favourite horse, Freyfaxi.

> I never want you to mount him, whatever need you may be in, because, as I have most seriously sworn, I will bring about the death of any man who rides him. Ten or twelve horses follow him. You are welcome to use any of these that you wish, be it day or night. Now do as I say, because there is an old saying, that 'he who gives warning is not at fault.' Now you know what I have stated. (c. 7, V 263).

This text, as everyone will recognise, recalls what God said to Eve – a point to which I will return. All is permitted to you, with one exception. Like Eve, Einar seizes the forbidden fruit. Hrafnkel keeps his word and kills him.

Since Einar's father, Thorbjorn, is a poor man, Hrafnkel ought to have nothing to fear. Hrafnkel's behaviour is always predicated on the assumption that power and wealth belong together. "Hrafnkel was often involved in single combats and never paid anyone reparation. No one received any compensation from him, whatever he did" (c. 2, V 262). But this one time he miscalculates. The saga is the story of this mistake.

Thorbjorn goes to visit Hrafnkel and demands his rights. Hrafnkel is aware that he has been very harsh in carrying through on his threat on the first occasion, when Einar has ridden Freyfaxi only a single time. He therefore offers Thorbjorn a generous compensation, something he had never done in this kind of situation before.

Thorbjorn refuses it and instead seeks help from his family. No one is very eager to take on a man of Hrafnkel's influence and attitude. But Thorbjorn does finally succeed in persuading his nephew Sam, a man – and this is an important point – who is learned in the law (c. 3). They set out for the Althing to bring the action. However it is not enough simply to be learned in the law; one also needs powerful people on one's side to have any hope of success. Sam tries to procure such allies.

> Sam sought out all of the chieftains and asked for their help and support, but they all gave the same reply. None of them felt that they owed Sam anything to make it worth their while entering into a dispute with Hrafnkel, and risking their honour. (c. 7, V 268)

In the meantime chance comes to his assistance. By means of some clever persuading, he succeeds in gaining the help of two powerful brothers, the Thjostarsons, from the other side of the country. Sam skilfully presents the prosecution's case at the Althing.

Hrafnkel has shown his contempt for Sam's attack by failing even to appear at the court. Why would he need to? After all he is the strongest. When he hears rumours at his booth that things are looking bad for his case, he decides — on the basis of his attitude to law versus power — to teach Sam a lesson, together with all the lesser folk who fancied themselves. He calls his supporters to arms:

> He intended to discourage small fry from prosecuting cases against him, and was going to break up the court, and drive Sam off the case. But this turned out to be impossible. There was such a crowd in the way that Hrafnkel could not get anywhere near. He was forced back by the sheer weight of numbers so he did not manage to hear the case of those who were prosecuting him. It was therefore difficult for him to present any legal defense for himself. (c. 10, V 272)

Hrafnkel is outlawed. Nevertheless this is not catastrophic. And not merely because of the legal technicality that the saga mentions — that the sentence of outlawry has to be proclaimed at his homestead before it comes into effect — but also because the society here, like that of all other sagas, lacks a police force. Since the value of a judgment is only as great as the power of those who can be called upon to enforce it, Hrafnkel accepts the one made against him with complacency.

But again he miscalculates. The Thjostarsons, who come from the western quarter, see their work through to completion. They travel east with Sam to Hrafnkel's farm and drive him off it with great cruelty by means of their superior numbers. Sam settles down in the empty farm and struts about in his borrowed plumage.

Had he taken Hrafnkel's life at this opportune moment, the saga would have ended there or continued according to the familiar pattern of family feud. But he lets him go still in possession of his life; and Hrafnkel, though destitute, can begin again in the neighbouring valley of Fljotsdal.

Here he grows rich and powerful once more. He sees Sam now and then, but neither of them reminds the other of their former differences (c. 13), until one day Sam's distinguished brother Eyvind comes home from abroad and rides past Hrafnkel's new farm. Hrafnkel sets out, keenly aroused by the time-honoured, proverbial, family wisdom, that a thrall woman utters. He kills Eyvind and drives Sam from his old farm, but lets him live. And Hrafnkel now settles down until the peaceful end of his days with two godords instead of one.

Concerning Hrafnkel's attitude the opening of the saga remarks:

> He was unfair towards other people, but was well accomplished. He forced the people of Jokulsdal to become his thingmen, and was mild and gentle with his own people, but stiff and stubborn with the people of Jokulsdal who never received any justice from him (c. 2, V 262).

To this is added the information already cited that he often took part in duels and never paid compensation.

The picture presented to us here is of a man of power. He divides and rules. He treats one group well and the other badly and thus avoids being considered alike among all. It does not come as a surprise to Sam that Hrafnkel has killed a man; he has heard this sort of thing about Hrafnkel before (c. 6). The law plays no part in Hrafnkel's conceptual world. He keeps his promise to kill Einar, not because it is a valid oath, but because he has got it into his head that he will keep the commitment he has made to himself. The saga's formulation could not be clearer. He does not keep his promise because of duty or tradition or some other over-riding imperative but because he was of "the belief that nothing goes well for people when the words of an oath come down on them" (c. 5, V 65). He does not give a damn about Sam's action at the Althing and that eventually costs him dearly.

When this happens, his character changes – or so some readers think. The saga says this about him when he has settled down in Fljotsdal to begin afresh without money or men:

> People talked much about how his arrogance had been deflated, and many remembered the old proverb, "brief is the life of excess." (c. 11, V 274)

Hrafnkel has not merely been humbled, he has also become humble in the view of these readers.

But just before this passage we learn that he has been able to buy his farm on credit. Now, putting on a humble face is surely a normal and often the only successful way of obtaining a loan, though it is obviously possible that Hrafnkel *has* actually learned humility. It is just that there are scarcely any indications in the saga that he acted humbly when it did not benefit him. Indeed he only acted humbly this once when it was the only possible way forward. His appearance now fully sustains the same interpretation as his appearance before. Now as before he chooses the expedient approach that advances his power.

The tactic works. Hrafnkel amasses wealth afresh and in time he thereby wins prestige in the district: "Everybody was glad to stand or sit, just as he wished" (c. 13, V 276)! There was a large immigration into the valley during this period, and Hrafnkel took care to control it. No one received permission to settle down peacefully unless they recognised him as their overlord. It is quite evident that he was both more popular and more sociable than before. But the saga writer is careful to ensure that we do not mistake this for a transformation. "He had the same temperament as regards his helpfulness and generosity" (c. 13, V 276).

Later on Hrafnkel's character ceases to be discussed. All that is mentioned is how he behaves: when the right moment comes, he avenges himself, not upon the little man whom only a technical error has made his equal, but on the little man's distinguished relative. Sam has to "content" himself with losing what he had appropriated. Hrafnkel retains both this wealth and the goods that he managed to amass during his period of humiliation, and he gains a lasting reputation into the bargain.

Hermann Pálsson, who has argued at length that the morality in *Hrafnkel's Saga* is Christian, has done so by showing the Christian ideas in the work and its verbal parallels with Christian texts. Undeniably both are present, but it does not necessarily follow from this that, considered as a whole, the image of life presented by the saga is especially Christian. Pálsson for example shows that the cited prohibition against riding Freyfaxi has its verbal parallels in the book of Genesis (Pálsson 1966, 30). But were this incontestable observation to be used as an interpretive key, then Einar would have to stand for sinful humanity and Hrafnkel for God, and what would happen then to the rest of the story? Pálsson's book about *Hrafnkel's Saga* suffers the basic shortcoming that it uses Christian notions to assess one or another episode but fails to explore the relevance of Christianity to the statement made by the whole saga. His book is a learned examination of parallels, which disclose the entirely unsurprising truth that the saga writer, who lived in a country that had been officially Christian for about three centuries, found himself in a Christian textual-world, whose formulae he drew on. Pálsson says nothing about what he did with the conceptual world of these texts.

The explicit religious dimension within the saga's fictional world has also been pressed into service in this discussion and not only by Pálsson.

Hrafnkel is called Freysgodi, that is to say, priest of Freyr, a most singular detail in saga literature. When he falls, his enemies kill the consecrated horse by sending him down to his divine owner, because "It would be most fitting that he who owns him should take him" (c. 12, V 275). Afterwards they desecrate Hrafnkel's temple to Freyr.

An assault on a heathen god and on what belongs to him can obviously function as a Christian act. That would be a possible way of interpreting it, were there no context within which to consider the act – but there is.

In the context of the saga the attack is seen, from the point of view of the attackers, as yet another humiliation of their enemy Hrafnkel. Freyr, as has been said, was a god one sees worshipped only very rarely in these texts. In this particular text, the cult of Freyr is very closely associated with Hrafnkel; a dishonouring of this cult is an attack on his worshipper rather than a missionary exercise. And from Hrafnkel's point of view, the event provides the occasion for an elaboration of one of the character traits we recognise in him from the rest of the story. His reaction, when he hears about the killing of Freyfaxi, is this:

> He then said that he considered it vanity to believe in gods and said that from that time onwards he would never believe in them. He kept his word and, after this never made any more sacrifices. (c. 13, V 276).

He conducts himself towards the gods as to the human beings: he makes use of them. What does not serve his ends, he has no interest in reverencing.

All this should not be mistaken for the prelude to an interpretation of *Hrafnkel's Saga* as a pamphlet against Christianity – far from it. It would be a Protestant way of thinking that would come to such a conclusion. The saga writer may well have been a pious cleric; if so, he surely knelt down to his rosary with perfect peace of mind after he set down the final period to his story of Hrafnkel, for it deals with something quite different from what the rosary deals with. It has to do not with a man's purification on his path to God, but with the mechanisms of power here in this world.

Nor is it a story of a human progress, though it has often been called such. It deals not with a character undergoing development, which would distinguish it from the rest of the sagas of Icelanders, but with an unchanging character, responding to *different* circumstances.

In this it differs from the long, richly populated, multi-generational stories like *Laxdœla Saga* and *Njal's Saga* since it includes neither a prelude about the golden-age law-based society in the past nor a reference to the Christian utopia at the end, such as is represented in the evangelical kiss between Flosi and Kari at the end of *Njal's Saga* or the purified anchoress Gudrun at the end of *Laxdœla Saga*.

It is a description of a society built purely on power relations without any idealizing embellishments. That the law has degenerated into being an ornament of power is not described as tragic chaos demanding a new order; on the contrary, it is seen as a condition under which the crafty can learn to thrive. The strong and the clever obtain justice, and God has certainly nothing against that: He it was, after all, who created cleverness and strength. In any case, the saga does not concern itself with the problem. Hrafnkel loses everything and gets it back twofold. But that is more through his own effort than through God's help. He is closer to a Krupp than to a Job.

Hrafnkel's Saga has been dated both early and late, and on the same grounds, namely its narrative perfection.

The romantic conception, that the sagas sprang fully formed from the soul of the people and thereafter degenerated, led to its being considered early. Its composition "forbade" dating it later than ca. 1200, wrote Finnur Jónsson in his literary history. If anything it is in his opinion still older.

The idea that saga poetics evolved slowly towards a culmination – the replacement of the romantic conception – leads to a dating at the other end of the period. Sigurður Nordal sets it in the final decades of the thirteenth century in *his* literary history. Pálsson (1962), in yet another attempt, wanted to place it in the middle of the century and to ascribe it to an identifiable author. But Nordal's dating continues to have its supporters and also fits well with the considerations here viewed as salient. Indeed it would be no surprise if the saga were still younger.

The struggle between conventions which is characteristic of the great sagas from the middle period of 1230-1280 has no place in *Hrafnkel's Saga*. We see in it neither the glorification of the past nor a utopian treatment of the future. The law is not in decay; it simply no longer functions as a means of obtaining justice; it serves only as an instrument of power.

As in the other sagas, violence is not the centre of interest. To be sure Hrafnkel's expulsion is a brutal scene: his hamstrings are pierced and he is hung from a beam so that the blood collects around his eyes. But of the death by which he avenges himself, we hear only indirectly: the story skirts the issue of violence quite consciously, by transferring the point of view to a servant who rides away from the battle, and thereby draws attention to the subtlety of the power play itself.

The saga takes less of an interest in the questions of *whence* and *whither* than do other sagas. It is chiefly concerned with the *how* of a new power-based society whose norms are static. The saga writer has no moral judgment to proffer against this society. He is far too enraptured with the delights of being able to describe its means and methods.

Hrafnkel's Saga is not a moral tale. Nor, to be sure, is it an immoral one. It is amoral, if we must define it in moral terms. It must have been written at a time when the question of social norms and their slippage was no longer a burning one. Christianity with all that it stands for in the Icelandic sagas – as we shall see below – is the obvious base, upon which the author can proceed to the real issue: the power struggles between men.

A late dating would conform to this reading of *Hrafnkel's Saga*. The story illustrates one possible version of the clash between the principles – longing for past justice and hope for new peace – which provides the philosophical foundation of the high classical sagas.

Grettir's Saga

The youngest of the sagas of Icelanders to be discussed here is the story of Grettir the Strong. It is supposed to have existed already in the thirteenth century, but the form in which we know it today is thought to have been written in the first quarter of the fourteenth century.

Not only in this study, but also in real life did *Grettir's Saga* occur towards the end. After this period the genre fell into decay and was replaced by romantic and fantastic sagas. Perhaps the analysis of this last great achievement can give an indication of why.

One notes that the sagas of Icelanders lie behind this saga like a fully inhabited landscape. They can be drawn on and referred to. Sagas about Njal, about the people of Laxardal, about Bjorn champion of the Hitardal people are all mentioned by name. Many others are alluded to.

The saga calls to mind *Njal's Saga* and *Gisli's Saga* in having only a single main character. But its form does not derive from these classical sagas with their structures built around a single turning point. Rather its form is episodic, like a string of pearls; thus it is more reminiscent of a pre-classical saga like *Eyrbyggja Saga*. All the same this saga does share one point of likeness with the classical sagas. Despite all its supernatural scenes, it aims at being "historical" in its appearance, containing as it does the conventional make-believe source-critical provisos: "without anyone knowing what he said," "without anyone knowing the cause of his anger," and the like. Apparently this is intended to communicate the impression that it has been possible to establish the truth of what we are told.

Internally *Grettir's Saga* differs rather importantly from sagas like *Njal's Saga*, *Laxdæla Saga*, and *Gisli's Saga* to the extent that it does not depict a society in dissolution or transition where different norms conflict with each other. This absence recalls other late sagas like *Hrafnkel's Saga* in its assumption of a stable society as far as social norms are concerned.

The conflict that the saga deals with arises – and remains – at the margins of society. The assumption that such margins exist, *Grettir's Saga* shares with other sagas and with much other medieval literature: beyond the confines of the social order chaos reigns; whoever drifts beyond the confines is struck by chaos. But Grettir does not drag chaos with him into society, setting off an avalanche, as we have seen happen in the classical sagas of Icelanders.

When characters like Bjorgolf in *Egil's Saga*, Thordis in *Gisli's Saga*, Halgerd in *Njal's Saga* or Hoskuld in *Laxdœla Saga* followed their own promptings, thumbed their noses at convention, and stepped beyond the pale of the ordered world, the catastrophic consequences spread widely within the social realm. Such does not happen in this saga. Going wild and transgressing boundaries continues to cause catastrophes, but almost without exception the consequences befall the uncontrollable person himself, who continually travels in the borderland, following his own head, fighting with berserks, bears, giants, trolls, and outlaws. But it is society that endures, and Grettir the strong who perishes.

Like *Laxdœla Saga*, the saga begins in the time of settlement and ends in a Catholic pilgrimage. But these two time periods do not unite to serve as a common point of contrast with the troubled middle period. The contrast is rather between a troubled and shifting ur-time, which is not conceived of as a golden age, and the actual time of the saga, which is that of a Christian society. Stable norms, understood to be self-evident, are well-established when Grettir enters the scene; only Grettir is unable to adjust to these norms. That is the essence of his story.

The past is depicted as extraordinarily turbulent. Vikings are defeated in their flight from Norway and move restlessly and aggressively among the islands westwards across the Atlantic until they settle down and find comparative peace in Iceland. Grettir is born here, one of two sons from his father's second marriage. Another son had been born of the first marriage but that constellation does not cause the trouble that we know from other sagas. The half-brother becomes Grettir's good friend and finally his avenger. The contracting of marriages occupies this saga unusually little. The source of trouble lies elsewhere.

To be sure, Grettir exhibits somewhat unruly behaviour in this area as well. On his first voyage to Norway, he would "much rather stroke Bard's wife's belly" (c. 17, II 72) than do his duty as a crewman, and during his outlawry three cases of erotic connection are recounted: with a half troll's lusty daughters (c. 61), with a well-established widow (c. 64 ff) and with a servant girl who did not think he was sufficiently endowed for such things (c. 75). But these relationships wreak no havoc. Their mention seems almost to be for the sake of completeness, to answer the inquisitive reader's question about how Grettir dealt with this aspect of life during the twenty years of his outlawry. The second of his three relationships produces a son, but he dies as a youth (c. 67). Other consequences do not appear. Grettir's erotic behaviour is more a result of his situation than its paradigmatic cause. It is more than difficult to determine what the saga is really saying about the origins of the unlucky pattern that imposes itself upon Grettir's life.

He has, to begin with, inherited a difficult character for which no clear explanation is provided.

His father sets him three tasks: to herd geese, to massage his fatherly back, and to tend a horse. He performs all three tasks equally badly and shortly afterwards he kills a man for a trifling reason. For this he is condemned to three years' outlawry.

Things might have continued in this way, but they do not. During his outlawry Grettir accomplishes good deeds, he kills bears and berserks, and struggles with evil spirits. He wins for himself great fame, which points to the fact that his unruliness can be channeled in ways that are useful to other people, if only he can be put in the right situation. The man who sails him over the sea from Norway grasps this and for the first time sets him on the right path. His father doesn't understand this, and sets him the wrong tasks, but his mother apparently does, for she says to the father:

> "I do not know which to object to more: that you keep giving him jobs, or that he does them all the same way." (c. 14, II 67)

But the outlawry is survived without any catastrophic results. And after three years in Norway, where Grettir is not made to herd geese, but is able to find expression for his abilities in great tasks, he returns to Iceland a respected man. True, he is expelled from Norway, but many have benefited from his abilities. His renown is great.

And yet he ends his life an outlaw. What is it that happens? The turning point comes when he meets Glam.

At the farm called Thorhallsstadir in Forsaeludal a haunting takes place which is so nasty that the farmer has difficulty getting people to stay on the farm to work (c. 32). He hires a sinister fellow with protruding eyes and wolf gray hair as a farm hand. This fellow, Glam, is good at the work but a heathen and no friend of the Catholic mass. Christmas comes and Glam refuses to follow the new custom and fast. On Christmas Eve he eats a full meal and goes out in ungodly weather. He never returns. He is found dead surrounded by footprints in the snow after a violent hand-to-hand struggle.

If the haunting before was bad, now it becomes worse. Glam comes back as a ghost and leaves no one in peace. Yet another fellow is killed in front of the farmer, who eventually has to leave his farm, until Grettir hears of the haunting and takes up the struggle. Grettir wins after much difficulty, but is cursed by Glam in the course of the struggle so that his strength will not develop to the extent it otherwise would have done:

> "You have become renowned until now for your deeds, but henceforth outlawry and killings will fall to your lot, and most of your deeds will bring you misfortune and improvidence. You will be made an outlaw and be forced to live alone and outdoors. And this curse I lay on you: my eyes will always be before your sight and this will make you find it difficult to be alone. And this will lead to your death." (c. 35, II 107)

The curse comes true, as such curses have a habit of doing. It is true that a brief and superficial account of the saga's conclusion would seem to indicate that it is a new magic unconnected with this curse that gets him in its power in the end. Grettir has entrenched himself with his brother Illugi and the thrall Glaum on the inaccessible island of Drangey. The period of outlawry is just at the point of coming to an end. It is his enemies' last chance to extinguish his life. After a vain attempt to climb the cliff from the sea, they seek help from an old troll-woman, who carves runes on a tree root, which floats out to Drangey. Grettir hews at it, but wounds himself on the leg, after which he becomes ill. With this, his enemies succeed in landing on the island and striking him down.

Yet this account is misleading. Grettir knows clearly that he should keep away from the accursed tree root. And he knows clearly as well that a watch should be kept at the place where the island can be breached. Yet when he fails to act on this clear knowledge at the decisive moment, it is not because of his enemies' strength but because of his own weakness on the island; he has fallen out with Glaum who despite a warning decides to hand him the tree root and does not give a damn about keeping watch. In the most profound sense it is Grettir's solitude, even surrounded by those with whom he has sought refuge, that brings about his death. Glam was right.

Among Grettir's forceful acts during his outlawry are many that serve to benefit Christian society. He kills a pair of giants who are making life unbearable on another farm, Eyjardalsa, and helps the mistress of the farm Steinvor over the river so that she can get to Christmas mass (c. 64 ff). It is again at the Christian festival that the haunting of the farm has become worst. Grettir stays at home on the farm and takes care of the heathen monster, while the Christians praise their God in church. Later he takes care of the giant woman's man, while the priest, who should have helped him, turns tail and runs. So Grettir helps to maintain the Christian order while he himself is condemned to stay outside it.

The judgment on him is moreover passed on the wrong grounds. On his second journey to Norway, right after his meeting with Glam, Grettir is stranded with his shipmates upon a deserted island without fire. He swims over an icy fjord and fetches fire from a couple of other Icelanders, the sons of Thorir from Gard. They are terrified when they see him coming out of the water, huge and all icy "like a troll" (c. 38, II 111). Drunk as they are, they begin to strike out and to flail about with burning logs. Grettir salvages some fire in a brazier and swims back. The following day the house where he sought the fire has burned down with the sons of Thorir inside.

This is the primary account of the event and hence the one in which we can have confidence. But a secondary one spreads about, first in Norway and later in Iceland, to the effect that Grettir has burned people to death without cause. For this he is condemned in Norway and convicted in Iceland.

In this distinction one glimpses a difference of degree between the two societies in which the saga unfolds. Norway is presented as an ideal state, the opposite of its treatment in the much older *Egil's Saga*. Here the Christian King Olaf rules, who gives Grettir a fair chance and lets him exculpate himself by means of a trial by fire. The trial fails because Grettir loses his temper while it is happening. Only then the upright king condemns him: "Rashness always breeds trouble. If any man has ever been accursed, it must surely be you." (c. 39, II 113). On Iceland conversely Grettir is condemned to outlawry purely on the basis of a rumour about the burning in, without his being present to defend himself: "Many people said that Thorir had acted more from zeal than respect for the law" (c. 46, II 119), reports the saga writer with one of those anonymous, indisputable judgments.

It is not possible to go beyond this single hint at a split between the two societies. The theme is not developed. The saga does not come to deal with the decay of Icelandic law and the transformation of an Icelandic society into a Norwegian one. It remains focused on the man who has to pay the price for the maintenance of an ordered society, and a high price it is. That the two societies on both sides of the Atlantic are and remain orderly is treated as a given.

This saga concerns itself as little as any other saga – and less than a saga like *Gisli's Saga* – with the personal evolution of a hero. Grettir may well suffer more and more as the years go by and the curse of solitude takes hold. But he does not go through a transformation that redeems him and then lets him die with a peaceful soul. He always acts in the same way and thereby fails to redeem himself. On the other hand he does redeem a great many others.

Read as a piece of human psychology, *Grettir's Saga* is jejune. The youngster we first meet is described as follows: "He was very overbearing as a child, taciturn and rough, and mischievous in both word and deed" (c. 14, II 64). He is troublesome to his companions first at home, later out in the world. And he is troublesome to himself.

On his deathbed, Grettir's father passes the judgment on him that "all his doings seem at the mercy of the wheel of fortune" (c. 42, II 115). This is not just a reference to the "Hávamál" (stanza 84), the wheel of fortune is also a well-known medieval image for the human experience that fortune's gifts are unevenly distributed. Grettir is an unlucky man. There is nothing more to say about it.

More interesting perspectives are opened if we see Grettir's ill-luck within the world in which it unfolds. His ill fortune is not dragged in among other people to the same extent as Gisli's ill-luck is laying life waste all about him. True, two of Grettir's brothers die, but his story does not become a feud story like *Njal's Saga*. Rather than engage in feuds Grettir saves many from ruin by his fights against berserks, giants, bears and monsters and, by doing so, he enables others to pursue an active and Christian life. Despite all his violence and strength, Grettir is not a destroyer but an upholder of society. Even his quest for fire, which unluckily causes men's deaths and his own condemnation, brings deliverance to others – his shipmates.

The conceptual universe that the saga communicates through this pattern yields the following lesson: the maintenance of society comes at a price. Society endures and will endure. But people like Grettir are needed to pay the price. It is a part of the order of things that one who struggles against disorder at the margins, one who has traveled out so far that he has directly confronted heathen forces like Glam – which is to say forces that defy societal order – such a one cannot return to society as if nothing has happened; he must remain an outsider. Grettir can bear Steinvor over the river, so that she can get to church, but the divine service may take place in peace only because he himself holds back from participating in it and remains behind to hold the evil forces at bay:

> Grettir was considered to have rid the place of a great evil. (c. 67, II 155).

Perhaps we may find a clue here as to why at this time the saga of Icelanders should be reaching its close as a productive literary genre. Its distinctive feature consisted in the analysis of the relationship between the conduct of the individual and the shattering of social norms. Sagas like *Egil's Saga*, *Njal's Saga*, *Gisli's Saga*, *Laxdœla Saga* build on the dramatic interaction between individuals and a society in the process of change.

In *Grettir's Saga* social norms are not upset, any more than they are in *Hrafnkel's Saga*. They are treated as givens. Interest is directed towards the exciting things that happen alongside the hedge around these norms and towards the exciting life lived by the men who stay on the outside and do the dirty work as proxies for the reader, who can shudder unconcerned indoors. We have left behind the descriptions of the struggle within society of the sagas of Icelanders. The path is cleared for the struggles of knights against dragons deep in the woods.

CHAPTER 6

THE SECOND PATTERN AND THE TIME OF THE SAGAS OF ICELANDERS

The Times

Having once read a series of sagas and discovered common patterns and myths in them, the next step is to find some point of comparison outside of the sagas themselves which will shed light on these discoveries. But what should it be? There is no agreement on this question. The absence of agreement depends on differences of opinion about the purpose of reading, interpreting, and exploring the sagas of Icelanders – and literature in general, for that matter.

In seeking to find a basis of comparison for the sagas of Icelanders we can turn to the times and the society they treat of. Ostensibly they describe Icelandic society as it was chiefly in the century 930-1030, which for the same reason is called the *Saga age*. One may ask: how well do they describe this society? To what extent do they provide an accurate picture, to what extent a false one? The last question obviously arises only when we cease to believe blindly in the sagas as history.

It is slightly less obvious that *all* these questions ultimately derive from the belief in the sagas as history. Doubt is only interesting during the period that immediately follows a time of belief. The period of belief in the historical accuracy of the sagas has long since passed, at least as far as the writing of prefaces is concerned and the enunciation of interpretive principles. But the attitude of belief lingers in the choice of the topics scholars have focused on and the methods they have used to treat them.

Certainly it would be of interest to determine how the image of society in the sagas of Icelanders relates to the actual conditions in the so-called Saga Age. In any event almost more interesting than to know how J.P. Jacobsen's portrayal of Marie Grubbe relates to the seventeenth century or Thomas Mann's image of Joseph and his brothers relates to ancient Egypt.

As far as the sagas of Icelanders are concerned, however, there is a snag to this line of questioning: what we know about tenth-century life in Iceland we know first and foremost from these thirteenth century literary treatments of it. Thus this method of inquiry involves a futile exercise: on the basis of one kind of subject matter – the sagas of Icelanders – we reconstruct another – the societal life they depict – after which we compare the two. It is hardly surprising that this circular procedure brings us back to precisely the point at which we began.

Another strategy is to try to identify the *authors* who wrote the sagas. This method is indeed familiar from other literary-historical studies, where it is more widespread than the approach described above. A literary historian will more frequently examine an historical novel in relation to its author than in relation to the period in which it is set.

As far as the sagas of Icelanders are concerned, there is a snag to this method as well, for we do not know who the authors were. The sagas have all been preserved anonymously. However, this has not deterred scholars, the search for authors goes on. And over the years names have been proposed for the composers of a good many sagas of Icelanders.

Agreement on the attribution of particular sagas is hard to come by, though. The most secure – to judge by the number of scholars who subscribe to the idea, not to mention the force and diversity of the arguments in favour of it – is the notion that Snorri was the author of *Egil's Saga*. Snorri wrote works in other genres: king's sagas and the prose *Edda*. We know something about the way he composed those works. Thus we come to know something about *Egil's Saga* – at least we gain food for thought – if we take seriously the possibility that Snorri wrote it.

But it is the exception. As a rule, unfortunately, the scholars who look for authors can only propose to us names of men about whom we know little other than the authorial conjecture now attached to them. Even this can be interesting – more interesting in fact than to learn that Homer did not write the *Iliad,* but rather another man with same name about whom we also know nothing. But if the proposed author is an unknown literary quantity apart from his name, the conjecture does not provide an occasion for much apart from the rather futile thought-process by which one reconstructs the personality of the author that the text may be supposed to reveal, after which one sets text against author and decides that they match.

Biographical literary scholarship, which seeks to identify the author as an historical person, suffers from the same weakness as the one based on subject matter. Both are limited by our limited insight into the processes that preceded the committing of the saga words to the parchment.

For all their inadequacies the two methods just described have been the ones more often employed than the two that will now be described. These share at least one common feature: the basis of comparison to which they have recourse can be documented and does not have to be reconstructed to begin with.

The first of these methods of proceeding, the third to be discussed here, develops out of comparative literature and asks what literature was accessible when the sagas of Icelanders were written, which works from other genres of Icelandic writing and from the European continent could the author have known and been influenced by? In brief what were the possibilities for literary *influence* available at the time and which of these possibilities are manifest in the sagas? We are talking here of an investigation into the other kinds of literature that existed in Iceland prior to and contemporary with the sagas of Icelanders, the kinds of literature created on the continent and finally the traffic in translations and ideas between cultures.

These three methods of going beyond the texts themselves in order to learn more about them have been outlined here in the briefest of terms. I shall talk about the actual conditions within the industry of saga scholarship in the last chapter of this book. For the moment what matters is to observe these methods of proceeding in their pure form, so as to be able to situate properly a fourth approach, which will be pursued here: reading the sagas in the light of the age and the society in which they emerged as fully realized wholes, that is to say, not the time they tell us about but the time in which they were written.

It follows from the foregoing that there are a number of questions that cannot be asked, namely the questions specified in connection with the first three approaches. It does not follow from this that these approaches should be rejected, even if I have to confess that there are some among them that I find less fruitful than others.

It may well be that there is much historically accurate information in the sagas of Icelanders. It could in fact scarcely be otherwise. It is also very possible that "the sagas" existed in oral variants, some – for example *Grettir's Saga* – in different written versions, in addition to those that we know. It is also probable, finally, that foreign literary exemplars were available to "influence" them. To the best of our present knowledge it is indeed very likely that this was the case.

But all these circumstances do not change the simple fact that at some point in time someone has written down a story that constitutes a unified whole – out of materials and forms found wherever – and that these coherent wholes answered to something in the time of the writer; how else would they have gained the resonance to which the count of different sagas and their numerous copies witness. Regardless of what brought them into being, the sagas of Icelanders were literary works that functioned in a particular time. The question that needs to be wrestled with is this: how were they able to function as they must have functioned? To what challenge did they respond? What was the relationship between them and the time and the social conditions in which they were given their now familiar forms?

Behind this question – towards which all the foregoing analyses have been moving – is the assumption that the sagas of Icelanders are works of art and that art is something other than meaningless entertainment; and that some analogy or congruence exists between the sagas and the time in which they functioned.

The art of putting this question effectively – here as elsewhere in literary studies of any period – lies in finding the proper level of abstraction. The difficulty in achieving this is perhaps one of the reasons why the question is as underexplored as it is.

In a lecture on this subject that he presented to a conference of Nordic philologists in Copenhagen in 1935, Einar Ólafur Sveinsson remarked that one has trouble imagining a scholar of the Icelandic sagas who has never felt tempted to ask whether a point of contact can be found between the saga writers' work and the time in which his work was carried out:

> Can that period be said in any way to be mirrored in the sagas, in such a way that they bear the impress of the time and place where they were written down? (Sveinsson 1938, 71).

But, he continues, having once asked this question, most people have also proceeded to set it aside again, perhaps because they viewed it as unproductive. With that he goes on to offer some suggestions which I will take up in my last chapter.

One understands very well that the question is discouraging. To be precise, it is not enough to be familiar with the sagas and to know a lot about the society of their time, the thirteenth century. A theory is also required as to what were the underlying forces at work in that society before a comparison can be performed which will not cause us to fall into one of two traps.

One trap consists in too low a level of abstraction. The numerous attempts to read the sagas as *romans á clef* is an example of this error. One identifies episodes belonging to thirteenth century history which are represented in a tenth-century guise and uses this information to decode the sagas. There is more value in such comparisons than in comparisons between sagas and the vanished time they purport to describe, for in contrast to the tenth century we know a good deal about the thirteenth century from sources other than the sagas themselves. But concerning the relationship between saga composition and the thirteenth century, we learn just as little by attending to the possibility that they are *romans à clef*. Similar results might be expected of strictly biographical literary scholarship, were it to be adapted to the sagas of Icelanders.

The other trap consists in too high a level of abstraction which ends up in the ether where everything is the same as everything else. The sagas deal with a crucial period of transition and the thirteenth century was such a time. But what period lacks crises and does not involve transition? The insights one arrives at by this type of inquiry bear on the universal human understanding embodied in the sagas, their insight into the truths of people's spiritual and communal life in all ages.

The sagas of Icelanders are well supplied with such wisdom, as is all literature of enduring appeal. But we also find in them answers to challenges specific to their time. Only by identifying those challenges – by, as it were, going through them and coming out on the other side – we have a chance of identifying what is truly universal in the sagas of Icelanders as an art form.

This is what we will now attempt.

But first some preparatory considerations need to be addressed. Before we can investigate what the operative forces and conflicts were during the period of the sagas, we need to spell out what we know about the dates at which the individual sagas appeared in their surviving form. I have long owed the reader such an accounting, for in the construction of the foregoing chapters, tacit assumptions have been made about the order in which they were written. Yet the sagas are characteristically silent not only about who wrote them but also about when they were written.

If despite all this we are able to arrive at some conjectural datings, we are indebted to the fundamental research that philologists have undertaken. Their work is the precondition not only for putting the questions to be asked here, but more generally for any literary-historical treatment of the sagas.

I noted earlier that the working methods that follow from conceiving of the sagas as history have survived in practice even after this understanding has been replaced – in theory, at least – by the conception of sagas as stories.

> The saga becomes historical when it does not originate from some poetic ground, but immediately takes form as an account of real events.

So writes N.M. Petersen in his literary history (1866, 204). And since, as we can see from his statement, he conceives of the sagas of Icelanders as belonging among the works of history, it is only reasonable that he groups them according to the region or quarter of the country in which their action takes place. There is more to be said about N.M. Petersen's conception of the sagas, however, a point to which I will return in the last chapter.

More debatable is the procedure used by someone like Jón Helgason in his own literary history (1934, 108) – a work incidentally that remains unrivaled until the present in certain respects, for example, in its discussion of style – based on the notion that the Icelandic saga "develops by degrees in the direction of the historical novel." Yet his hesitation in breaking with the traditional conception is understandable at a time when there were still not the number of attempts to date the sagas' composition that there would be in 1953, when Sigurður Nordal came to write *his* literary history, which was the first to attempt at a comprehensive account of the Icelandic sagas according to their supposed date of composition, rather than the geographical locus of their subject matter. His result shows how difficult the task is.

Nordal begins persuasively with a chapter about six sagas reckoned to belong to the decades 1200-1230 and continues with a chapter about twelve sagas thought to have been written in the period 1230-1280. At this point the procedure begins to blur. The next five sagas are placed between 1270 and 1290 (or 1260-1300) and the fourth group is located in about the same period; the reason for considering these latter as an independent group is not the time of composition but the mode of composition. There follows finally a fifth group from 1300 and after.

Although the criteria of division are temporal, they do not result – as first appearances might lead us to believe – in five time periods, but rather in four or even three. And if we pay attention to all the stated opinions as to when each individual saga was composed, the number of periods comes dangerously close to one.

Thus as far as dating is concerned we are still on uncertain ground, although much less uncertain than fifty years ago. In the foregoing I have in individual instances cited the differing estimates, which show how difficult it is to place the sagas on a time line.

For all that, on the basis of internal features and supported by the scholarship just referred to, I have ventured to assume the existence of three periods.

The central one is the middle fifty years of the thirteenth century, during which a number of high classical sagas were very probably composed. I have attempted to separate out some earlier sagas which according to common opinion stem from the beginning of the period or just before it, and which consistently differ from the sagas of the central period in some basic features. And I have done something similar at the other end of the period. But it is very possible that *Eyrbyggja Saga,* which is here viewed as pre-classical, was written later than *Egil's Saga*, which is classical; or that *Hrafnkel's Saga*, which I treat as post-classical, on grounds mentioned in the analysis above to which I will briefly return, was composed before *Njal's Saga*.

When literary-historical periods are defined by reference to basic attitudes and styles of writing, they never match neatly with the calendar. In this respect there is nothing unusual about this genre or period. Nor indeed would the problem be solved by analysing all the sagas of Icelanders rather than only a handful. It is not quantity that determines the characteristics of a period's literature, rather it is its best literary works.

What our analyses have shown is that among a number of the longest and best sagas from the classical period, we can identify two types of causes for the bloody and tragic conflicts. That is, in addition to the first pattern, which has always been acknowledged and is therefore not discussed here, consisting of the drive for achievement and the appetite for wealth and honour, there exists a second pattern based on the erotic drive, which – whether freely acted upon or thwarted – may set in motion sequences of events catastrophic to the small society in which they take place: collisions between rules – whether legal or customary – and individuals who transgress the rules.

The preceding analyses have also shown that the sagas at issue are informed by a fundamental understanding of society, an Icelandic myth as I have called it, concerning a period of decline between two high points, a state of conflict in which two sets of social conventions struggle with one another – one, harking backwards, the society of law, and the other, the society of mercy which is imagined and hoped for in the future. Each of the high points represents an ideal, but when things go badly, during the fallen stage between them, nothing remains of either apart from a pale afterimage or premonition.

Furthermore the analyses have shown that some sagas can also be found in which the motif of love and the motif of social conflict are indeed present, but in which they are not woven together into the skein of causes found in the classical sagas, and that subsequently some sagas can be discovered wherein social norms remain fixed, where the second pattern disappears and where the writer's interest turns towards the mechanisms of power within the static society or the repressive struggles at its margins.

I am not claiming that this description can account for all sagas of Icelanders – even if it can certainly account for more than those dealt with here. Nevertheless, rather than documenting this last claim with a few catch phrases about a handful more sagas of Icelanders, I will turn my attention to the question that the sagas already analysed provide adequate grounds for raising.

What have these traits to do with the time of the sagas? To what challenges do they supply an answer? It is very possible that the ingredients can be traced to continental literature; the manner of their combination belongs exclusively to Iceland of the thirteenth century. To be influenced by is not the same, finally, as to copy, rather it is to be helped in responding to some of the challenges that have to be faced when, as an author, one is attempting to deal with the task of formulating one's conceptual universe or philosophy by means of a narrative.

Histories and Two Historians

According to the *Saga of Thord Kakali* the priest Eyvind Thorarinsson attempted to arrange a reconciliation between a certain Gisli and a certain Kolbein who had participated in the killing of Gisli's close friends. Gisli must swear fidelity to Kolbein. Needless to say, this does not appeal to Gisli. The priest thinks about it for a little while. Then he tells Gisli that he himself has a son named Kolbein; Gisli needs only to think of him when he swears fidelity to "Kolbein." Gisli does this and no one sees through the prevarication.

In *Gissur's Saga*, we learn how the title character arranges a marriage of reconciliation between his son and his enemy's daughter. During the wedding feast, Gissur holds peace talks and, as the guests are leaving, he tells two of them, Ari and Eyjolf, that they must come and visit him again. They promise to do so. And they keep their promise: not long afterward they return to burn Gissur and his family in, like Njal at Bergthorshvol.

Sagas like these two distinguish themselves from the sagas of Icelanders in that their material is not derived from, or transferred to, the tenth century. The two episodes mentioned take place in the 1240s and 1250s. These sagas were written down at the same time as the sagas of Icelanders, which means that only a short time intervened between the occurrence and its reporting. These two sagas together with many others have been gathered together and adapted in the composite text known as *Sturlunga Saga* because its principal subject is the first two-thirds of the thirteenth century, the Sturlung age. It is the fundamental tenor of this period that one perceives running through the work and also through the two episodes which I have chosen at random from among many similar ones.

They are linked by their common focus on promises and on a somewhat unusual manner of keeping them. They do not deal simply with promise-breaking. Literally speaking, the two prevaricating parties who make the promises keep them, it is just that they attach to their words a meaning very different from the one understood by those to whom the promises are made. As readers we witness a discrepancy between the content and the expression of language. We see with our own eyes the decay of the very institutions of negotiation and agreement that were fundamental to a society like that of Iceland during the free state era, which – lacking a central executive authority – depends on the respecting of agreements and the keeping of promises. The forms are still in place, but they have become empty.

As we know, the Sturlung period ended with the dissolution of the Icelandic free state and the country's complete submission to the Norwegian crown in 1262 and the years immediately following. Episodes like these and many, many other similar ones from the multifarious *Sturlunga Saga* create a propensity in the reader to focus on the moral dissolution to which they witness and to attribute to it a decisive meaning with regard to the political changes that were coming about.

Against this, historians of widely differing persuasions have raised objections. We will examine two contrasting examples in an effort to penetrate more deeply into the heart of the matter, the latter on the basis of an explicit theory concerning the lawfulness of the society, the former without such a basis.

Einar Ólafur Sveinsson, to whom frequent reference has already been made, has written the longest and richest work on the age of the Sturlungs (1940), which title it bears. His study comprises a series of chapters dealing with free retainers and royal subjects, class and wealth, vices and virtues, entertainment, death, twelfth-century Christianity – as many aspects of life in the Sturlung age.

The first thing that Sveinsson mentions in his prologue is the "disastrous" subjection to a foreign power: "that great tragedy tinges with sorrow all our ideas about this age." One does not need to read further to discover who "we" are: the present-day descendants of the Sturlung age. It is an Icelander who is writing, and he does so as a party to the matter. He goes on to sadly identify the many moral charges that are laid against the age of the Sturlungs, but also proudly refers to the enormous cultural activity of the time, of which the sagas of Icelanders, our topic, are only a part.

> The contrast between conscious, disciplined cultural achievement and the frenzy of unrestrained vitality is the outstanding characteristic of the age and the riddle of its life. (7)

He describes in a short and schematic fashion the most important political events on the path to the fall of the free state. Finally he sets himself the task of coming a little closer to a solution of the riddle. We will attempt, he says, to grasp the fundamental temper of the people of that time, "the changes in outlook and habits of thought and the forces underlying these changes" (7).

The reader will not be mistaken if he feels the energy that has fueled this exercise more fully present in the opening lines of the prologue than in its concluding lines. Throughout the entire book, one is aware of a desire to rescue the Sturlung age from moral condemnation.

What we must not forget, according to Sveinsson, is that sagas about this period "omit to speak of those affairs which were carried on in a lawful and peaceable manner; these were not *söguleg*, not worth telling about. A cursory reading of *Sturlunga Saga* may therefore easily give rather a misleading impression of the life of the time" (26).

In contrast to certain other scholars Sveinsson wants to see the period from within (63). Nevertheless the comparative dimension is not absent from his thought. The age has been reproached for the looseness of its sexual morals. In contrast to the Renaissance what happened was quite innocent, he claims. In fact, according to Sveinsson, as regards morals the people of the Sturlung age could essentially hold their own against any other ruling class in any other period.

> Certain other periods have kept their offences of this kind more to themselves, but the claim of hypocrisy to count among the virtues is not incontestable. (63)

He considers other sins and always comes to the conclusion that they were also committed at other times, or that the *Sturlunga Saga* also offers examples of the corresponding virtues. He points out examples of the condemnation of sins by people of the period itself, and he enumerates sins such as poisoning or contract killing that seldom or never occur in the thirteenth century (70). In brief, the Sturlung age has no reason to reproach itself.

Yet pernicious forces are also to be observed in the period, he grants. The church, which is praised for contributing a number of good influences, is not entirely a source of benefit. Within literature it happens that the style of Old Icelandic in the oldest written works from the twelfth century and the "pure and limpid classical saga style, which thus belongs to the Sturlung age" contrast favourably with a clerical style which in the hands of monks and energetic clerics follows at the heels of foreign models: "long-winded rhetoric and sentimental prolixity" (117). "It is quite possible that some of these works were written by churchmen, but if so, they did not write them as churchmen but as sons of their people" (150). "They have seen and heard fully as much as they relate, nothing is seen through the cloister window or from a distance" (152). The Catholic Church, according to Sveinsson, was not the beneficial force in Iceland that it was in other European countries.

When he comes to his final assessment, Sveinsson refuses any attempt to reduce the period to a simple formula. The Sturlung age was more than anything else a complicated and variegated time "a powerful and grand symphony played by a large orchestra" (153). No instrument, no voice is missing in this contrapuntal music. What was described as a riddle in the prologue has become a musical composition by the conclusion of the book.

Sveinsson's book is itself an orchestral work in which many instruments and voices can be heard. One learns much about the Sturlung age from a man who has come to empathise with his subject through long study and sympathetic affection and who knows it inside out. But we will understand fully what he has to say about the coherence of the Sturlung age only when we see his book *The Age of the Sturlungs* in its context. Like all orchestral works it has – despite the richness of its swelling chords – a theme.

The theme is this: the people of the Sturlung age were sufficiently good; there is no reason to feel inferior just because one descends from them. Other countries were indeed no better, and furthermore some of the ills of the age came from other countries. No less than the sagas of Icelanders, Sveinsson's *The Age of the Sturlungs* contributes to the interpretation of Iceland as a nation. Like them it participates in the creation of an Icelandic myth, which is to say the idea that moral qualities can be attributed to an age as a whole rather than simply to individual actions. Thus despite everything, the book has an ideological basis in this sense: a set of ideas that furnish a basis for value judgements.

For all his dismissal of formulae, Sveinsson comes close to one in the last lines of his book: the introduction of the monarchy was "one of the main causes behind the collapse of the old civilization"(153). This is directed against those who believe that the causal sequence was the reverse. There remains however a third possibility, that both developments, which undeniably occurred, had still another shared cause.

Einar Olgeirsson tells the story of the Sturlung age from a different angle. He too writes from an ideological base in the sense just explained. Unlike Einarsson, he draws attention to what it is, if not in a programmatic prologue, then in the value-laden title of his book which might be translated as "Family Society and State Power in the Icelandic Free State" (1954) and especially in the theoretical literature it builds on, Engels's book about the origins of the family, private ownership and the state (1884). It is an effort to describe Iceland's early history in Marxist terms. Olgeirsson's Marxism however has a strongly national cast.

Olgeirsson brings a world-historical perspective to his vision of the revolutionary change of Iceland from a free state to a part of a kingdom in the memorable year of 1262. Family societies are to be found everywhere in the pre-historical period. Roman civilization, with its bondage and slavery, is overrun by the family society in the form of a movement that historians have commonly called "the Germanic migrations" but which Olgeirsson prefers to call "the greatest revolution in human history" (19).

But at the moment of this victory, the family societies entered their final phase. They were not made to be ruled or to rule. Olgeirsson sees this drama re-enacted in the Old Norse myth of Sigurd, who kills the dragon Fafnir, while the dragon guards the gold, and thereby brings about his own destruction. "The workers' movement of our time needs to recognize its kinship with the heroes of the old family society in their struggle against the curse of gold" (25). Family societies are slowly superseded across the face of Europe. The survivors are driven towards the northwest, while a class society and royal power arise in the voids left behind.

The large-scale emigration to Iceland, which takes place in the decades around 900, is part of this struggle. The settlers attempt –

successfully – to recreate a polity in the form of a family society on the uninhabited Atlantic island, and they are successful in resisting the pressure from Norway right up to the Sturlung age. Then the collapse occurs in Iceland too. The triumph of feudalism is now complete.

If the temporary recreation of the family society succeeded in Iceland while it failed for the vikings in Normandy and England, the reason is clear: Iceland was uninhabited, there was no peasantry to subjugate. A rational argument this, except that other notes creep into the account which agree poorly with the dialectical-materialist analytical base, whereas they agree rather well with the familiar notes struck by saga scholars and historians of a different persuasion.

Those who emigrated to Iceland were "an energetic and powerful and uncorrupted barbarous farming people from the Nordic family society" (67). They loved two things: work and peace (68ff). Through their poetry we gain an insight into "the high and healthy ethic, the mature, unspoiled moral sense that is embedded in the breast of family heroes, as they confront their destruction" (27). The family society is a "classless" society (30) and it was re-established as successfully as it was in Iceland thanks to the settlers' "wisdom and sense of justice" (82). Slave owning is naturally a stumbling block in this interpretation, but there is "no doubt that slave owning declined quickly in Iceland, even from the very beginning of the age of settlement," in Olgeirsson's view (128).

Perhaps to the readers' surprise, he welcomes the introduction of Christianity, but this is because it was a very "heathen Christianity or Christian heathenism" (213) that took root in Iceland, diametrically opposed to the Catholic Church's institutional oppressiveness on the continent.

The family society is Olgeirsson's moral yardstick. It and the people who belong to it are the more perfect the further back one goes in history and the fewer the sources that witness to how it actually appeared. In its original form, it was communism pure and simple. There were no tyrannical rulers only elected kings, who led it. Its most perfect expression is unfortunately to be found in the pre-historical period. Regrettably the societies we know something about are all less ideal. But that is because the family society was in decline throughout historical times. Its final collapse marked the introduction of the class society, the society in whose final period we now find ourselves. It just remains for the reader to conclude – though Olgeirsson does not spell it out – that where the classless society endured longest, it may also re-emerge earliest. The people of medieval Iceland had all the requisite qualities. Why should their modern descendants not possess them as well?

Where is it that we learn of this cycle – if not in *Laxdæla Saga*, *Njal's Saga*, the Icelandic myth of the classic sagas of Icelanders! Olgeirsson's book is based on the same golden age model as they, like so much thinking once again in the nineteenth century and its spiritual inheritance in the twentieth century: There was once a golden age, which has been lost to us, but it will come again, if only we do the right thing.

There is a profound difference between the points of departure in the thoughts of the liberal Sveinsson and the socialist Olgeirsson. If the chasm between their books does not feel quite as deep as that which separates their departure points, that is because they both share in the Icelandic national consciousness which bridges the gap. They proceed down different paths, but both come to boost the national past. It is almost as if Olgeirsson too attributes to the Norwegian king's power-lust a primary role in the fall of the medieval Icelandic free state. In any event no king is ever mentioned without a morally disparaging word thrown in.

Olgeirsson concludes his discussion of the Sturlung age with a suggestion as to how *Njal's Saga* can be read as the saga about the fall of the family society. In this, I believe, he is right. But I think too that one can advance further in one's understanding of the saga.

It is not possible to utter any objective truths about such matters. If the sagas are to be read in their societal context, a theory of the operative forces in society is required, for the reading depends upon it. On the other hand, one can safely withhold judgement on the question of whether the thirteenth century in Iceland or the tenth-century family society should be rated high or low on the moral scale.

Let us make an assumption. Let us suppose that it was circumstances at the very foundation of Icelandic society that determined the conditions of which saga writers acted as interpreters. The assumption is related to that of Olgeirsson, but differs decisively from it, because – among other things – it does not partake of the presupposition that the historical family society is the ideal classless state. The foundation consists then of a number of facts selected as follows.

Iceland was settled in 870-930 by migrating Norsemen who arrived in a country where conditions remained good for a long period. Settlers were able to take all the land they could work. The result of the settlement was a society comprising many farmers who did not differ as much in terms of land ownership, and therefore power, as their descendants would later. They created a polity that consisted of a legislative and judicial authority, but no executive or central authority to rule and punish. This structure was possible because no enemies were gathered at their borders to attack them and because power was distributed relatively evenly among relatively many.

Not among all, of course. There were, whether one likes it or not, slaves and poor people alongside the great farmers. The extent of the democracy was hardly greater than in ancient Athens. But the great farmers were sufficiently numerous to hold one another in check and to ensure that any freeman who had gained a legal judgement in his favour could reasonably hope to find an ally to assist in its execution.

The balance that this unique social structure presupposes went to pieces in the following centuries. Ever more land and power were gathered into ever fewer hands after the country was fully settled. At the beginning, farmers could choose for themselves which of the godi, or chieftains, who eventually numbered 39, they would be "in thing with," that is, whom they would choose as their chieftain. A godord was thus from the beginning partly a voluntary association of men, not a district. But this is what it gradually became. Taxes began to be levied, so it became profitable to be a godi and in consequence to sell godords.

Fewer men possessed power in the country and foreigners gained control over external trade. All-powerful, wealthy families arose in the thirteenth century and conflicts between them gradually assumed the dimensions of a real war. A change had come in the conditions of production, by which I mean in the ownership of the means of Icelandic production – land and cattle – and the distribution of the products. With this there came a change in the nature of the conflicts.

But the institutions of former times continued to exist. The absence of a central authority and of a police force remained unchanged. The social order in the Sturlung age still depended officially on family solidarity and on the ultimate force of laws and agreements in settling cases, although the basis for such a social order had weakened. It was thus not a question of immoral magnates or of a power-hungry king, it was simply a question of time, how long the surviving social institutions could endure – always in accordance with the assumption spelled out above. In 1262 time ran out.

The strokes of this sketch are very broad; doubtless there is much in it that needs correction. It would require a whole book – and an historian – to complete the design. Instead we shall turn to the question of how the sagas of Icelanders interpreted these conditions. The greatest among them are not simply descriptions of this social transformation, they also present an interpretation of it and of the role of the individual within it. Their interpretation differs from that of Olgeirsson and that of Sveinsson. And also from my own, as spelled out above.

The Conceptual Universe of the Icelandic Sagas

Thorolf Kveldulfsson died, that was where we began, so we can begin our summing up there.

He faced a king who was in the process of using force to create a new feudal society. Thorolf's family stood as representative of the old kinship society that was being destroyed in the process. Old Kveldulf advised his son to stay clear of King Harald Fair-hair. But Thorolf submitted voluntarily to the king's command and obtained a distinguished position in the new order. For all that, he fell beneath the sword of royal power.

Thus read this is the story of the violent meeting between two kinds of society. Thorolf did not manage to survive it. But his nephew Egil Skallagrimsson, who takes up the quarrel with the royal power in an enlarged form, holds his own on the strength of his manliness, and cunning. A piece of Icelandic history extolling the national past in the description of a hero.

But if we read the story of Thorolf in the manner that has been attempted here, it points in a different direction. If we ask how the narrative lays the causal groundwork for the death of the noble man, the answer is *not* that he confronts a power-hungry king who uses any ignoble trick to extend his authority. The narrative is laid out to ensure that the reader can follow the motives of every single one of the actors from the limited point of view of each. If we attempt this with respect to King Harald, we will find neither ignobility nor lust for power behind his conclusion that Thorolf's days should be numbered. He is put in a situation that makes his behaviour reasonable, indeed his only reasonable choice.

The sons of Hildirid are the ones who created the situation. They make use of trickery that neither Thorolf nor the king would have thought of using. They are creatures of a lower rank in the social and moral order.

But the saga does not stop there, stigmatizing the sons of Hildirid morally. The saga makes it possible to evaluate *their* motives too in relation to their situation. And, according to this evaluation, they too behave reasonably: they have been placed outside society and have no other way of entering into it – and into their father's inheritance – than through intrigue.

Responsibility for their way of acting therefore falls finally on the one who put them there, old Bjorgolf, who late in life is inflamed by a lust that he does not curb in accordance with the behavioural norms of the time, a compulsion to which instead he immediately gives himself over when he forces Hildirid's father to make over his daughter on his own terms. In our unraveling of actions and motives, we came to a halt with this compulsiveness unchecked by social sanction. And we found that the saga did not engage in the relations between the two individuals, but focussed on the consequences for other people of the way the two entered into their relationship.

With this single action in contravention of the customary order a grain of sand is introduced into the delicate social machinery. And this grain of sand is enough to cause catastrophic consequences for innocent people in a quite different part of the machine. The fulfilment of desires laid the groundwork for a second pattern which can be discerned in the story beneath the first pattern of opposition between men jealous of their honour. The latter is the means whereby the conflicts caused by the second pattern are transformed into actions.

What is anticipated in *Thorolf's Saga* comes to fruition in the saga it is the prelude to, the saga of Egil Skallagrimsson. In it both kinds of motivation combine in one person, the impulse that does not conform to the ordered life of the community and the power struggle.

Egil's first great disappointment is that he does not get the girl he wants. The saga depicts this very discreetly, yet clearly. The day the disappointment is sealed – the day his brother marries the girl – he meets the woman who represents dangerous erotic power in this saga and others, Queen Gunnhild. He commits a desperate act compelled by the situation he finds himself in and thereby furnishes the king with a motive for becoming his enemy, strongly urged on by the queen. In this way a polarization, which has its root in individual compulsiveness, is carried forward into the time of the saga, where it conditions all the decisive conflicts that follow.

Egil holds his own in the struggle. He is no Bjorgolf. He knows how to channel the disparity he feels between his urges and his scope for action into positive acts that compensate for those that are denied him. The most famous example in the saga of him saving himself by transforming disappointment into an action that enables him to carry on is the poem "Sonatorrek," which he composes in response to his son's death. But the personality trait of which it is the expression shows itself in many other places in the saga. Egil's world avoids collapse, even if his urges cannot be conformed to his possibilities. For the same reason the world around him does not collapse.

However, a collapse does befall the world – which is to say the human society – in which the subsequent sagas take place. Like the beginning of *Egil's Saga*, the beginning of *Laxdœla Saga* includes many examples of the contracting of relationships with an emphasis on the legal and customary aspects of such transactions – in stark contrast to what gradually unfolds in the main action.

Hoskuld drops the first grain of sand into the machine by acquiring a concubine's son, as it was termed. This was legal from a technical, juridical point of view. But, as the saga shows, it was not conducive to the peace of the family, which Hoskuld also endangers in another way by behaving unjustly towards his brother. What these two sequences of events have in common is that he does not show the same unconditional respect for the unity of the family as does the generation dominated by the ideal female settler, Unn. This saga too concerns itself more with the consequences in the society around Hoskuld, than with Hoskuld's own state of mind.

Things do not go catastrophically wrong, because his actions are contained by the powerful forces of conciliation nearby. But the efforts at reconciliation begin to seem uncertain. Olaf Peacock, who is a man of peace himself, brings the conflict to a crisis through his own well-intentioned peace-making efforts, which destroy Laxardal in the third generation. This is a motif that will reappear with much greater consequences in *Njal's Saga*. As in *Egil's Saga* it is the conflict between erotic urges and their possibility of finding a proper expression – within the Kjartan-Gudrun-Bolli constellation – that creates the most dangerous problem in the saga.

In this it resembles much other literature. Its distinctive feature in relation to literature dealing with similar constellations – both distant works like Oehlenschlager's "Kjartan and Gudrun" from the nineteenth century or nearby ones like the prose version of "Tristan and Isolde," which existed in Old Norse when *Laxdœla Saga* was written – is that the saga takes only a limited interest in the beautiful and rare emotions experienced by those who play out their roles in the love-triangle, and focuses almost exclusively on the chaos that the love triangle causes among the people connected to it.

In *Gisli's Saga* the connection between erotic activities and chaos in society is subtle. It is not just Gisli who dies, an entire family is so utterly destroyed that the on-going lives the saga ought conventionally to conclude by describing have to be reduced to one family member – the youngest Sursson, Ari – who has played no part in the saga since its beginning; had this Fortinbras participated more fully, he like the others would very probably have become contaminated by the chaos that is introduced.

The cause of this havoc is the jealousy between two brothers, once again a quite personal state of feelings which is analysed not for its content so much as for its consequences. But the havoc is also the result of two different ways of relating to conventions, which in this context means states of society. And these two ways reveal themselves in relation to erotic conduct.

When Thordis, the sister of Gisli and Thorkel, endangers the family's good name by blatant erotic conduct, however much or little actually lies behind this conduct, Gisli knows only one solution: the sword, whereas Thorkel understands something different: to make accommodations.

The contrast is repeated later in the saga before and during Gisli's outlawry, to which Thorkel also knows how to accommodate. One develops a keen respect for the whole-hearted Gisli; but there is no getting away from the fact that, given the way people behave, including for example Thordis, Gisli's whole-hearted behaviour has a way of making what is bad worse.

Gisli's Saga depicts a society adrift. Some time-honoured rules run amok and drag the society, whose rules they were, to destruction. This happens most clearly in the saga about Njal.

Njal's Saga makes less of its pre-history than does the saga about the people of Laxardal. It begins when the collapse is well underway. People like Halgerd and Hrapp, who yield without restraint to their own personal urges, whether erotic or otherwise, thereby set a light to the fuse that leads elsewhere in the society they inhabit. It is thus a society of unexploded mines. The explosives are the product of, among other things, the growing discrepancy between law and society, between jurisprudence and justice.

Njal attempts with all his might to establish peace. He advises Gunnar as to a technically correct procedure which nevertheless produces treacherous consequences. And he advises his countrymen to institute a court of appeal, in order that he can advance a move in his own reconciliation plan by means of this newly-established institution. But, as he suggests, the procedure, which is also technically correct, has disastrous consequences. The society's juridical superstructure, as a result, has become a bit more complicated. In the new legal maze the settlement goes astray.

The world described by these sagas is immoral in the sense that actions do not measure up to declared or unspoken principles. According to the sketch of the saga's time of composition presented in the earlier part of this chapter, this should not take us by surprise. The peculiarity of these sagas is the interpretation they provide of this discrepancy in society.

In all the major sagas of Icelanders the disasters may be traced back to a discrepancy between the impulses that individual people experience and the bounds that society has laid down for their expression in action. Where an impulse is followed regardless of whether it runs counter to family interests, society is shaken to the core either on the spot or much later somewhere else. Chaos comes of love.

From this one might conclude that the saga's image of life builds on a moral judgement. However this is misleading. It is only exceptionally and where the saga is weakest that the root of evil is seen as malignity and nothing more, as in the case of Valgard the Grey, whom Unn marries, bringing wickedness into her family.

More frequently the people who start the avalanche – Thordis in *Gisli's Saga*, Bjorgolf in *Egil's Saga*, Hoskuld and Gudrun in *Laxdœla Saga* – are not judged, but merely described as being the way people are. What these sagas of Icelanders tell us is that society and the individual are so constructed that they do not always mesh. The result is not so much morally reprehensible as tragic; it is not so much caused by evil design as by – to introduce at last a word that many have doubtless long awaited – fate.

Writing so many pages about the sagas of Icelanders before introducing the word 'fate' is surely an experiment never previously attempted. There exists an extensive, even copious literature dealing with the Icelanders' idea of fate, as this is expressed in their sagas. A variety of words are used in the sagas to refer to the concept of fate that occurs in most of them. Much can be said about this, if one attempts to enter into the spirit of the age, to understand it from within, as if one inhabited their conceptual universe.

Which we do not. But fortunately it is also possible to conceive of it from the outside insisting that we are and must remain readers who inhabit a different conceptual universe than that of the sagas, and who come to the sagas as readers from the outside. Seen from this perspective their concept of fate is the result of their psychological interpretation of a discrepancy that, as I understand it, had roots other than psychological ones.

Wherever the concept of fate occurs throughout the world, it serves as a name for the power that impels what cannot be explained in any other way. Fate is a name for what is left over, a residual notion. When the interpretive models available to people are adequate, that is to say when they are constituted in such a way that they can account for a large portion of the problems that confront people, there remains only a small residue to which the term fate can be applied. When the opposite is the case, the time may be termed fatalistic.

The period before the thirteenth century I shall leave aside, since it is not part of the discussion. But during the Sturlung age, the time in which the free state collapsed and the sagas of Icelanders emerged, the unaccountable residue was large and the weight carried by fate commensurately heavy, for what the anonymous saga writers did was to interpret a transformational process, which had deep social and material roots, in individual moral and psychological terms.

It is easy to be wise in hindsight. We know, as the Icelanders did not, that the process of transformation their society was going through – and the discrepancy that consequently arose between their institutions and their daily life – was part of a universal pattern. The old law had to be violated for the simple reason that a new one was in the process of creation, not because a certain king wanted it or because another farmer was a nasty fellow. Since it happened all over Europe, it cannot have been the responsibility of any single individual. But the authors of the sagas of Icelanders had to see it that way, because they could only catch a glimpse of the scene that we can now survey more fully. As a result much remained to be ascribed to fate, for conflicts that were rooted in society and its material conditions were interpreted as if their roots were in the individual.

Then again, that is a distorted picture of the sagas. The peculiarity is not that they moralise, but that they moralise so little. Their singularity lies not in the frequency of the references to fate, but in their infrequency. The sagas never isolate the individual although they portray the flaws of society as deriving from the individual. They focus rather on the interplay between the individual and those among whom the individual is situated. They are concerned with results in one place produced by causes in another. They constantly attend to the role of the individual in the struggle between order and chaos in society.

In some of the richest sagas of Icelanders – *Laxdœla Saga* and *Njal's Saga* – the transition from heathenism to Christianity stands in the centre of the story. To read the sagas of Icelanders consistently as an interpretation of the time during which they assumed their finished form as works of art is not to assume a slavish correspondence according to which this religious transition occurred only in the thirteenth century. This transition had happened many years before, officially by means of a decision of the Althing in the year 1000 (or the year before). The sagas were written in the Christian era.

But the final transformation to the social form that Christendom had gradually assumed on the continent took place during this period. The year "1000" in the sagas is a symbol for "1262" in the real world, if these two dates can be permitted to stand as convenient abbreviations for the entire complex of transition. In the sagas of Icelanders, we find a myth about a cyclical movement from an ideal state, the old society of law, through a period of division and decay, to a new ideal state: the new, hoped-for, Christian society of mercy, which is the conceptual superstructure for the situation in which conflicts are no longer resolved by the individuals involved, but from above. But the narrative centre of gravity of the classic sagas lies in the stage that intervenes between memory and hope.

Both before and after the period in which the high classical sagas emerged, we found sagas that depart from this structure.

Among the early works, stories of various kinds occur: in one, for example, individual conflicts stand at the centre without any particular consequences for the society they take place in – thus *Kormak's Saga* – in another, bloody feuds occupy the interest more than the connection with their specific causes – *The Saga of Bjorn Champion of the Hitardal People* – while yet other sagas like *Eyrbyggja Saga* are of an episodic, tale-telling character.

At the other end of the age of saga composition we encountered sagas in which the social situation is no longer treated as a problem in the same sense that it is in the classical sagas. The society pictured in *Hrafnkel's Saga* has settled into a power balance pure and simple – and unadorned. The interest is turned towards the way in which a man gets along in such a society. *The Saga of the Sworn Brothers* is a comic version of the same basic social ideas.

In *Grettir's Saga* no violent social disturbances are caused by the hero's flaw. He himself rather than others must pay the price of his ill-luck. Conversely Christian society is the better for his presence. He is available to struggle against the heathen powers that threaten it, and thereby to ensure its continued existence. Its stable existence is taken for granted. The transition has been survived.

The literary-historical progress that becomes apparent in this simplified model reveals a genre that came into existence on the basis of a large and incomparably rich narrative tradition, whose transmission *before* it was transformed into written literature is set aside in this discussion. We began with the fact that the sagas that survive do so because they were written down. And we have discovered in them a number of topics that gradually blend together into a myth of the country's history and into an analysis of how and why this history progresses towards its crisis and then towards the hope that there is a way out of this crisis.

The development of the genre reveals constant raids into the realm of the inexplicable, which is termed fate, in the form of an inquiry of epic character into human actions and into their consequences and motivations. It is simple enough for a later period, that can see the age of the sagas of Icelanders in perspective, to detect the limitations of this inquiry. It is more difficult – and more useful – to use this insight to see more clearly the relationship between one's own time and the corresponding role that literature may play in it.

The role that the sagas of Icelanders played in *their* society was to embellish it. When one is surrounded by hateful murders and inadequate laws, it is easy to fix one's gaze on a time when killing was the work of heroes acting justly with a quick blow in the name of the law. That is obvious and easy to understand.

It is, however, not the whole truth about the function of the sagas of Icelanders. They cannot so simply be dismissed as escapist literature, for their principal subject – or, more accurately, the principal subject of the classical sagas – is not the age of heroes, but the age of collapse. The noble and upright time is the point of departure, but all the energy is spent on the investigation of why the collapse took place. The result they arrive at can be summarized in the following formula: a discrepancy arose between people's make-up and the make-up of society.

As regards the individual the outcome is a moral assessment. But as regards society it is the rare insight that the social order is not necessarily part of the natural order: society can be organized in *different* ways, and when one way fails to work any longer, it is time for another.

Those of the sagas – *Laxdœla Saga* and *Njal's Saga* – that complete the mythic cycle end in a situation where the family society dissolves and is replaced by a society where every individual is directly subject to a higher power. In the language of the sagas – and the understanding of the saga writers – this power bears the name of the merciful Christian God; in the everyday realities of life and the flow of actual historical events, this concept was represented by the power of the Norwegian crown.

It is often said that the sagas of Icelanders look backwards. If we take them at their face value, this perception is incontestable. But according to the reading presented here, they are equally a progressive interpretation and a welcoming of the historical change that was underway, which thirteenth-century Icelanders struggled against in their conscious actions even as they were bringing it about through discrepancies within their own society.

They saw decay around them, and used their literary works to interpret it as part of a mythic cycle. Their circumstances led them to glorify their originary period, but also – and here their genius is manifest – to push as far as they could their analysis of discrepancies that they saw about them, and furthermore to set out their hope in the future, in a new, purified state. The Icelandic myth was the response to a psychic need in their struggle for self-understanding. The sagas of Icelanders delivered the answer.

The end of the Sturlung age and that of the period of saga composition occurred when a new order was forced upon the Icelanders from the outside. That meant the end of a literature that had addressed itself thoroughly to the question of the individual's role in society. Only then, but then indeed, the function of the sagas of Icelanders became escapist. The myth lived on – in sagas that have been copied and recopied, and in other guises until this very day, as we have seen.

No one can dispense with a philosophy of life, a conceptual universe. One of the functions of a literature is to give it form. Few have been endowed with a literature that penetrates so deeply into the great problems of life as the Icelanders of the thirteenth century. They could not dispense with their myth. But the saga writers did not escape the uncomfortable problems in the dark portion of the mythic cycle when giving the Icelanders their myth. On the contrary they turned most of their energy to its illumination, as far as their light carried.

Continuations

To anticipate others let me be the first to admit the limitations and simplifications in the model proposed here. Yet it ought to be discarded only if – but then certainly – another equally simple model better deals with the facts. We understand through models, whether we admit it openly or not, and models always simplify.

Let me be the first to acknowledge as well what the table of contents has already made clear, that not all the thirty something sagas of Icelanders are dealt with here. This is not a study of the Icelandic sagas nor of *the* Icelandic saga, but of the conceptual universe to be discovered in a number of major Icelandic sagas. There are some that fit the conception sketched here only poorly, even if there are also many beyond those I have discussed here that fit it well.

I have briefly sketched out how I understand what was happening during the period of saga composition, the thirteenth century, not because I believe myself to possess the final truth about what the history is all about – any more than about what the sagas of Icelanders are all about. The material is inexhaustible and the work continues. At most this is but a small step forward. What I have suggested is a provisional but coherent understanding of the sagas of Icelanders, one that I think merits discussion – hence this book. I have sketched my understanding of the historical context to which I see the sagas as belonging, so that readers may know my prejudices. An essay like the one presented here depends on its author's idea of the period that is interpreted by the literature under discussion, whether this idea is acknowledged or not.

We could proceed by reprimanding the ancients because they interpreted the conditions of the period differently, but that would be foolish. I have not written a whole book to announce that a modern has a different view of the past than its contemporaries had; such a point could have been made more briefly.

It would make much more sense to proceed – while simultaneously researching the saga's sources, literary influences and loans, possible author identifications, etc. – to proceed with the reading of other medieval works from the same standpoint: what interpretation of the period of writing do they contain through the adaptation of the historical – or "historical" – material that they make use of, what conception of life do they present and what challenges does this respond to?

From this perspective we can read the other Icelandic saga genres: the kings' sagas, whose historical reliability was, curiously enough, doubted before that of the sagas of Icelanders (see Paasche 1922), the bishops' sagas, mythical-heroic sagas, contemporary sagas, knightly sagas. Even so historical a work as the last part of Saxo Grammaticus's *Gesta Danorum*, written not very long before these works, invites a reading of this kind.

If it is doubtful that we can learn much history from works that present themselves as history, it is certain that by reading works in this way we can learn much about how the age of writing was experienced and interpreted by the men who wrote them and by those who – as readers or listeners – could make use of them.

This is not to say that nothing of the sort has been done before, only that much remains to be done. And not just in medieval studies. A perspective like the one proposed here may be applied to works of many genres and ages. John Ford's westerns, for example.

CHAPTER 7

BOOKS ON THE SAGAS OF ICELANDERS

We can begin where we left off on the first page, with Carsten Hauch.

The proposal made on the previous page – that we should approach demonstrably historical literature in the same way – essentially originates with him. Hauch ascribes to epic literature goals identical to those that he, as a Romantic, would ascribe to history. Both kinds of activity seek to unravel the innermost connection between events mutually and between events and the human soul. It is the Romantic poet speaking here. History and poetry and fiction (and other forms of art) are different incarnations of the same ideal: Truth.

In the period following Hauch, a sharp division was drawn between fiction, conceived of as invention, and history, understood as the science of how things really were. Today it is once again possible to see the kinship between history and poetry and fiction, not in the Romantic way as revelations of Truth, but as different expressions of the truth about how people in a particular time have interpreted their circumstances – with the help of fiction, that is "poetry", or by means of the selection and ordering of the facts about the past, that is "history." Between now and then research has been based on the indubitable distinction between the two, between what is historical and what is literary in the saga, in other words, into what constitutes "free-prose," and what "book-prose," to use the standard terminology of saga scholarship.

The primary debt of gratitude owed by anyone who studies the sagas, regardless of scholarly orientation, is to the philologists whose industrious efforts over the generations have produced the editions upon which all discussions depend.

We are likely to forget this. But if we recall the state in which the sagas have been preserved – in incomplete, scarcely legible manuscripts containing divergent texts – we will appreciate the endeavour of the philologists the better. It is easy for a poet like Johannes V. Jensen, in the preface to his translation of *Egil's Saga* (1930), to scoff at the learned "with mouse nests in the hair" (18) who have watched over the sagas. Nevertheless, the pre-condition for his work and the work of all the others who have translated, distorted, discussed, erected theories, and extracted conceptual universes is that the painstaking guardianship has been performed. All work on the sagas rests on the philologist.

We know Hauch's work on *Njal's Saga* for it was published in 1855, but the manuscript of his lecture seems to have disappeared – at least no trace of it can be found in the archives. These do, however, preserve a letter from N. M. Petersen, one of the spokespersons for the "Historical School," translator of *Historiske Fortællinger om Islændernes Færd hjemme og ude*, that is "*Historical* Accounts of the Icelanders Travels at Home and Abroad," and author of *Den oldnordiske Litteraturs Historie*, in which the sagas of Icelanders feature as entirely historical accounts. In his letter of 14 May 1855, he thanks Hauch for sending him the printed Njal lecture:

> In my opinion there can be no doubt that the best sagas are historical novels, and it only remains to prove this historically. But what will the Icelanders say to this? It will be a while yet, before this new notion clears a path for itself, but it will, and new light will be shed on the development of Icelandic literature. (Ny. kgl. S. 3751, 4° I)

This is astonishing. Is N. M. Petersen contradicting himself for politeness's sake in a thank-you letter? Or is Hauch's conception, despite everything, not as unprecedented as it has been made to seem in the history of saga scholarship? The answer to both these questions is perhaps no.

The point is that N. M. Petersen, like Hauch, is a child of Romanticism. In his literary history (1866), where, to be sure, the sagas of Icelanders are treated as very historical, one finds phrases that match Hauch's almost to the letter: "The Word has two manifestations: poetry and history" (182). The deep division between the two kinds of writing belongs to a later period. For N. M. Petersen, as for Hauch, the task of the historian is to discover the "idea of the time":

> An idea reveals itself in narrative. It becomes critical history through historical art. The saga becomes history. (N. M. Petersen 1866, 182)

Thus there is not quite the inconsistency that first impressions led us to suppose between N. M. Petersen's historical conception of the sagas and his approval of Hauch's poetical conception. And by virtue of their common point of departure in Romanticism, it is scarcely as surprising as one might suppose that Hauch should conceive of the sagas as fiction. It is Hauch's qualities as a literary critic rather than his conception of the sagas that makes his treatment of *Njal's Saga* unique.

Romanticism has coloured much of the past for us. This applies also to a large extent to the problems of the saga age. But on this one point there are grounds for believing that Romanticism is more closely akin to the thirteenth century than is the age that followed it. In contrast to post-Romanticism, the thirteenth century – like Romanticism – apparently did not conceive of history and poetry or fiction as sharply divided; as far as they were concerned, both fictional and historical narratives were "sagas". The inclusion of a story-teller's idea in historical narrative did not render it untrue, and such untruths hardly made it poetry. To be sure these are surmises. But their basis is the fact that the Icelandic language did not distinguish between the two kinds of narrative, see for example Steblin-Kaminskij (1966). I dare say that saga research since Hauch and Petersen has done this – and so monotonously that this opposition has come to dominate most of what has been discussed concerning the sagas for more than a century.

What will the Icelanders say about this? asked N. M. Petersen. The Icelander Finnur Jónsson (1858-1934) spent his life answering this question. And his answer to the idea that sagas were novels was, "Rubbish!"

> However boastful it may sound – I will maintain and defend the historical reliability of the sagas, until I am forced to lay down my pen. (Jónsson 1921, 141)

The debate about the sagas has been fought out in rather violent duels over the years. Perhaps the reason for this is that the quarrels have derived their energy not merely from love of truth and from the struggle for academic prestige – as would be normal – but also from nationalist feelings. Treating the sagas as works of fiction "only" and not as history struck the descendants of the saga folk as a devaluation of their national history.

And if, into the bargain, the sagas did not arise from native origins, but had literary roots on the European continent, this struck some as a radical diminishment of the Icelanders' past. When the Belgian Bley (1909) wrote a whole book arguing that *Egil's Saga* was a literary rather than an historical work, Finnur Jónsson came close to saying "so's your mother" in his response:

> In my opinion, the whole book is nothing more than a fundamental misconception ... It is pointless to be more specific about this work which should be considered more as fiction than as science; there is not a single assertion that cannot be effectively challenged. (Jónsson 1923, II 407)

This was all the argument that Finnur Jónsson felt he needed to mount in order to dismiss Bley. Even among humanists this is coarse porridge.

The tone has not become less emotion-laden over the years. During the 1960s, a discussion took place between supporters of the "Icelandic School" and a representative of the "European School" – which designations will be explained shortly. Finally in the debate the point at issue became whether Swedish Radio had approached someone to present his point of view or whether it was he who had approached the radio! Saga scholarship is not only uncommonly comprehensive. It is also uncommonly emotional.

It is not my purpose here to give a complete account of this research. Rather this discussion is intended to trace as many lines through the material as are needed to place the foregoing work within the traditions of scholarship.

The *dating* of the sagas, which is the precondition for – and consequence of – some of the later disagreements, is itself a bone of contention, for even this question is not ideologically neutral.

National Romanticism's bequest to Icelandic philology consisted in complete certainty as to the reliability of tradition and a belief in the origin of the sagas among the common folk. The authentic Romantic idea about the identity of history and poetry and the deeper truth in both, on the other hand, got lost. The national dimension of the heritage was emphasized, rather than what was truly Romantic in the original sense of the word.

Finnur Jónsson's view concerning the dating of *Hrafnkel's Saga*, referred to in the chapter on that saga, is an illustrative example. Whereas later scholars no longer under the spell of the national

Romantic inheritance consider it to be late, Jónsson considered the saga early because of the high quality of its narrative artistry. In his view, if the saga arose among the common folk, the effect of literary reworking would be to contaminate its original purity. The oldest are the best and the best consequently the oldest.

Fortunately there are many other and better indicators on which we can base our judgment. These may be found carefully enumerated in the prefaces to the individual critical editions that will be discussed below. A comprehensive treatment of those arguments that may be useful in arriving at a dating, and the basis of my own discussion above, is found in Sveinsson (1958).

The *book-prose/free-prose* discussion has been conducted in major works by Liestøl (1929) and Nordal (1940). It has also been reflected in discussions of a variety of specific and isolated problems. Jónsson's angry note to Bley is one such instance. Bley's arguments build on, among other things, the question in Chapter One above concerning the inheritance of the sons of Hildirid. This question has been discussed in saga scholarship in terms of its legal ramifications. Bley took a different view from that of his predecessors, a fact of limited interest.

What is exciting is that he was able to perceive the source of their disagreement. His opponents were Jónsson and Maurer, two of the most prominent supporters of the sagas' immaculate historical conception, while he himself believed that *Egil's Saga* at least is a work of fiction. In this discussion, Bley came to conclusions about the law which support the interpretation of *Thorolf's Saga* presented above. But our views diverge again in the interpretation of Egil's relationship to Asgerd (Bley 70, for example).

A counterpart to Bley's book is found in Vogt (1901), who also treated *Egil's Saga* as a work of creative fiction, written by an author. Although Vogt's study has little to tell us today, it was a pioneer work in its time. Free-prose theory received its classic formulation in Liestøl (1929). Book-prose in Nordal (1940).

All of this will be passed over in great haste, mentioned for the sake of good order and because it leads us to the four "schools" that will be described below.

We have been able to follow the debate between book-prose and free-prose at a respectful distance. It is fair to say that for the moment the former position seems to have achieved a certain ascendancy, though with many qualifications and nuances depending on the scholar in question and the saga at issue. The four schools that I am about to describe – all of which naturally take positions within the book-prose/free-prose debate – make up the immediate background of the study that I have presented in the preceding chapters.

The only one of them whose name has not been invented for this occasion, since it is the name in common use, is the *Icelandic School*.

Under the leadership of such scholars as Sigurður Nordal and Einar Ólafur Sveinsson, members of this school have pursued a literary approach to the sagas in stark contrast to earlier Icelanders such as Finnur Jónsson. Its proponents belonged to the book-prose school and considered the sagas as works of art, which they explored one by one, investing much energy in efforts to identify the anonymous authors. A major achievement of this school was the creation of the Íslenzk fornrit editions, texts whose critical introductions were their showcases.

The best example known to me of an author-identification that the school proposed – even if it did not receive Sveinsson's approbation – is Bardi Gudmundsson's attempt to ascribe *Njal's Saga* to the already mentioned Thorvard Thorarinsson (1958). The burning-in at Flugumyr in *Gissur's Saga* in the 1250s is the key phenomenon here – the model for the burning at Bergthorshvol. Pálsson's first book on *Hrafnkel's Saga* (1962) is another example.

That the school was created in opposition to the exponents of the historical saga schools may be observed in Nordal's epoch-making book on *Hrafnkel's Saga* (1940), which is compelling as an argument against the belief in the historical reliability of the saga, but which has less to offer when it comes to viewing the saga as a work of fiction.

Sveinsson advances further in this respect in his book about *Njal's Saga* (1943), one of the triumphs of the Icelandic School. The book consists of a series of chapters which deal with one or another feature of the saga, its "roots", its "artistry", the description of characters, the individual characters of the saga, the philosophy which, according to Sveinsson, first and foremost involves the notion of good luck and ill luck. Sveinsson is deeply – and catchingly – convinced of the artistry of *Njal's Saga*. To cite a summary expression of his thesis about *Njal's Saga*:

> Why did the author write this rather large work? I am afraid that you will not find my answer profound: *in order to tell us a good story*. Give me an eye to see and a tongue to tell of what I have seen, the Icelandic novelist Halldór Laxness said somewhere. This applies uncommonly well to *Njal's Saga*. (Sveinsson 1950, 18)

The efforts of the Icelandic School have meant a big step forward in the scholarly understanding of the Icelandic sagas since Jónsson's day. But, like all views that are enunciated in polemics, those of this school were determined by the stance of its adversaries, though this was not as obvious to them and to their contemporaries as it has since become.

Hallvard Lie (1939), who has written what is probably the most detailed and critical characterization of the school in a review of one of the introductions to a volume in its series of saga editions, points out one example of this: their overwhelming preoccupation with chronology, a subject which ought to be of scant interest if they really trusted their own conviction that they were dealing with works of fiction, not history.

Yet another consequence of the impact of their adversaries is that members of the Icelandic School did not have much to say about the specific artistic features of the sagas; they were so preoccupied with insisting that the sagas are fiction, not history, that they did not get far beyond calling them "good stories." They were engaged in a polemical war. In a war, you are concerned with winning, not with nuances and corollaries of your own position.

To a large extent they won. They enabled us legitimately to regard the sagas of Icelanders as works of artistic, literary creation – and left it to us, their successors, to spell out the theoretical and analytical consequences of that view.

They certainly did not include among their primary interests the utilisation of comparative literature's classic implement: the investigation of influences. Perhaps this can best be understood on the basis of some features of the school that Lie describes so neatly and approvingly in connection with the great saga editions:

> And behind everything one notes the warmth of the feelings that sets the undertaking in motion and also ensures its fortunate conclusion: love of the land that gave birth to the sagas and of the people who inherited and who own them. (Lie 1939, 97)

The land that gave birth to the sagas has also nourished them. It is only human to be uninterested in knowing whether one's mother has had a foreign lover. Unlike the Icelanders, however, European and American saga scholars of comparative convictions have had much to say about such foreign, i.e. European, flirtation.

The basic text of what might be called the *European School* of saga criticism is a brisk essay by Paul V. Rubow (1928), which happens also to be basic for the Icelandic School. That both schools should be indebted to this one essay by Rubow is a result of the fact that it at once argues that the sagas of Icelanders are novels – an idea that the Icelandic School developed further – and alleges that these novels are inspired by medieval French novels, more specifically the romance of Tristan and Isolde, which was translated into Old Norse by a certain Brother Robert in 1226. This Robert, according to Rubow, can thereby be said to have laid the foundation for saga composition.

The Icelandic School in the proper sense of the phrase has largely let this last, comparative claim go unnoticed, unlike scholars of the next generation. The keen interest in influences from European continental literature has been taken up both in Iceland, by people like Bjarni Einarsson (1961), and abroad, by people like Lars Lönnroth (1965, 1976). They have not paid special attention to the Tristan problem, but they share a common interest with Rubow: that the sagas of Icelanders have to be seen in the context of a literary evolution, even if this point of view results in granting that literature has influenced the sagas, which are then no longer as "Icelandic" as they used to be. This view is perceptible in many places in 20th century scholarship: in the work of Turville-Petre (1953), in *Norrøn Fortællekunst* (1965). An overview of the research into the European literary roots of the Icelandic sagas is to be found in Tveitane (1969).

I have already stated the reasons why the present study is neither in agreement with nor at odds with the European School. We simply ask different questions and for *that* reason get different answers. This can be made a little clearer if we use Lönnroth's dissertation (1965) as an example.

This work is a summary of four articles whose common impulse is the wish to show that what is considered peculiarly Icelandic is in no way peculiar to Iceland. Ancient Icelanders did not distinguish – as did their very nationalistically minded followers, we may infer – between translations and originals. Nor did the distinction – alleged by, for example, Sveinsson – between secular and spiritual culture exist in Iceland. In brief, Iceland was a medieval country similar to other countries in the Middle Ages. Its literature developed from that of other countries.

In conclusion, Lönnroth mentions the original features that remain unaccounted for once one has found the source of this, that and the other.

> Unfortunately it is not possible for a literary historian to elucidate such original features. He can only describe the tradition and influences that have formed their basis. (Lönnroth, 1965, 25)

In other words, answers tend to be echoes of the questions one asks. Lönnroth and I have simply asked different questions; the sagas have responded accordingly. There is doubtless much wisdom to be had from the examination of the literary influences which the Icelandic school made too little of, according to the Europeanists. But there are other ways of putting questions to the sagas of the Icelanders that are at least as legitimate.

One of those whose legitimacy is open to debate is that exemplified by Hans E. Kinck (1921) and Hallvard Lie (1946). Two is a little too few to constitute a school, but let us nevertheless for the sake of this summary accord them this honour. And since they are both from Norway, let us call it the *Norwegian School*.

Hallvard Lie's treatment of Egil – however one regards it – is among the most excellent studies in the rich literature devoted to Egil. Lie's purpose is to explore

> What it was that drove Egil to this exceptional journey (namely the voyage to York)? In this question, as far as I can discern, lies the central problem for all Egil research, since it turns on nothing less than a psychological exposure of the characteristics of the "saga hero" and the skald. (Lie 1946, 155)

This is a programmatic statement through and through. The proper line of research is one of tracking and revealing hidden psychic forces. In this Lie's work is very much akin to a literary analysis. The problems he concerned himself with are the problems a literary analysis encounters along its path. I owe Lie a debt of gratitude.

And yet we are headed in two essentially different directions. The psychic forces that Lie wants to uncover are indeed so well hidden that they have escaped the saga-writer's attention. Nor are they rooted in the saga-writer's subconscious. In short, they have no place in either the tale nor in the teller of the tale. Where then? Well, in our good old friend from the days of the historical school, the real life hero of the tenth century, the skald whose historical life is portrayed – and distorted – in the saga, hence the quotation marks around the "saga hero".

According to Lie, it is possible to gather objective evidence from the saga on which to base psychological judgements that differ from those of the author. In such instances the analyst is right and the author of the saga mistaken!

What we have before us in this Norwegian work is, on the one hand, questions and concerns that are quite central for the literary analyst and, on the other hand, a work very much in the tradition of Finnur Jónsson, for it trusts the saga as history and proposes to uncover a reality – albeit a psychological reality – behind the work of art – albeit a reality which the artist may not have been able to understand.

Hans E. Kinck has done something very similar in "Et par ting om ættesagaen. Skikkelser den ikke forstod" – "Characters the saga did not understand" (1921). The two Norwegians are at once extremely aestheticist – in their subject matter – and extremely historicist – in their belief that the characters in the sagas are distorted versions of real people.

Lie himself defined the two ways of reading, his own and the one that I have attempted. If we want to read the sagas with "sober historical intentions," that is to say in order to get to the bottom of "the historical realities that provide the basis of the sagas" (186), we must entirely eliminate the "subjective element" introduced by the author, that is to say we must see beyond the distortion that is introduced, for example, by Snorri, the rational saga-writer, who is limited in his ability to understand the not nearly so rational Egil. This is what Lie does. If on the other hand we approach the saga as art, we must submit ourselves attentively and sympathetically to the author's artistic plan.

I owe the Norwegian School a debt, but what I have learned from it I have used for purposes that differ from theirs.

The last group of works to be mentioned can scarcely be called a school for their authors come from different countries – especially Germany and the United States – and they have lived and written at different times. A designation along the lines of the *Ethical-Aesthetic School* will indicate what they are about for they are concerned with such issues as ethics, morals, fate, dialogue, composition – issues that presuppose that the saga should be treated as a literary form rather than as an historical document; issues that turn the attention inwards towards the individual saga, away from the question of authorship, which preoccupied the Icelandic school, and the question of influence, which preoccupied the European school, and with important exceptions, also from questions about the rise and fall of the saga considered as a genre.

A classic in this field is the Swedish poet and scholar A. V. Bååth (1885), who analyses four sagas of Icelanders and comes to the conclusion that the notion of fate is the cement that binds individual parts – novella-like episodes or, to use the Icelandic word for novellas, thættir – together. He is one of those, including Hauch, who analyses the consequences of Njal's advice.

There are studies of dialogues by Jeffrey (1939) and Ludwig (1934) and also studies of morals by Toorn (1955) who singles out three phases of ethics in the sagas of Icelanders, but characteristically does not put them into any context once they are pinpointed. Many of these works proceed by isolating categories of a formal aesthetic or ethical nature and then searching the saga for examples.

Concerning fate, there are a series of treatments of which a remarkable one is a chapter on this subject in Brøndsted (1958), which comes to the conclusion that fate in the Icelandic sagas is not "an unyielding goddess who exists outside of humankind, but a mysterious power in man, distinct from his will and bound up with his lineage" (159).

A number of analyses of individual sagas are available, especially in German, for example on *Gisli's Saga*, Prinz (1935) and Seewald (1934). The most comprehensive study is Andersson (1967), which attempts to establish a structural model for all sagas of Icelanders. This structure comprises: 1. Introduction, 2. Conflict, 3. Climax, 4. Revenge, 5. Reconciliation, 6. Aftermath. It is not surprising that the pattern fits most sagas. Translated back into plain prose, it involves no more than two statements: 1-3 and 6 inform us that the subject matter is epic narrative, which has a beginning, a climax, and a conclusion; 4-5 inform us that what is special about this genre is that it includes acts of revenge. So what we learn from this is that sagas are stories of blood and vengeance.

What is valuable in Andersson's book – and it is a valuable book that has been very useful to me – is not this piece of theory but the twenty-five summaries of plots of as many sagas. It must have been yet more difficult before this book existed to work systematically and comprehensively with many sagas, for it is unbelievably difficult to keep their many similar characters and situations straight. Andersson has produced a useful manual to assist overloaded and feeble memories.

Finally it is possible, as has been attempted here, to try to understand the sagas of Icelanders as literary works shaped under particular historical conditions. This is an obvious consequence of the issue of the long struggle between book-prose and free-prose. The conclusion has been long in coming, but it has arrived at last, despite all reservations and nuances. Nonetheless, the results have still not been pursued far enough to allow us to talk of a school.

Many researchers are convinced that one or another feature of the sagas originated more in the thirteenth-century than in the tenth century – their Christian character, for example, according to Baetke (1952) and Schomerus (1936). This is in direct descent from the Icelandic School's efforts.

It is also from this school that impulses emanate to proceed further. It was Sveinsson (1940) who wrote the previously discussed book about the Age of the Sturlungs, and it was Sveinsson (1938) who, as mentioned, presented the proposal to a congress of philologists that we should attempt to see the sagas as an image of the period in which they came into existence rather than of the period they purport to describe.

Like other members of the Icelandic School, Sveinsson harboured a distrust of totalizing viewpoints. Even the question of the sagas' degree of artistry or historicity, of which the school had an almost doctrinaire view, had to be investigated anew for each individual saga, a conviction that they emphasized time and again (see, for example, Nordal 1957).

Furthermore, the position that Sveinsson advocated in the lecture just referred to becomes a call first and foremost for detailed investigations of limited questions. The first result of this call in the lecture is the identification of the younger Bolli's vengeance in *Laxdœla Saga* with an event in 1244, which is narrated in *Thord Kakali's Saga*. Such procedures have led to the identifications of authors and to the discovery of *passages-à-clef*.

But Sveinsson also hints at other ways of proceeding. He outlines the stages in the country's common history – as opposed to an interpretation that focuses on the different histories of the various regions – during the period in which the sagas were written. And he proceeds to the questions: by whom and for whom were the sagas written? Did the saga writers have a purpose, and if so, what was it?

Sveinsson steers the questions in the direction of the wish to know more about the individual authors and the particular districts. The sagas are separated from each other like individual people – each tells its own story and has its own history.

This way of looking at the sagas prompts an interest in the age of the Sturlungs. Without historical knowledge about that period it is impossible to go further in this direction – Sveinsson (1940), R. G. Thomas (1950).

But the questions that Sveinsson has raised may lead not only to the individual and the particular but to enquiry into the interdependence between texts and epoch, between the sagas of Icelanders and the 13. century in general. The sagas may not be historical source-texts, nevertheless – like all other imaginative literature – they are historical phenomena that can better be understood within their historical context.

Baetke (1956) has picked up the thread in a book whose title – *Über die Entstehung der Isländersagas* – recalls some earlier works, but whose opening points in a different direction.

> Literary works arise on the base of particular societal and cultural conditions at a particular period; they are created by people whose lives are played out within the limits that these conditions define and give expression to these people's opinions and strivings. (Baetke 1956, 6)

To employ this program on the sagas, Baetke feels obliged to clear the ground, that is to say, once again take up and go through the free-prose/book-prose discussion. There remains therefore scarcely so much room as the opening leads us to expect for the analysis of the sagas on the suggested basis. Saga people, Baetke says, are in no way autonomous individuals, but are seen as mutually dependent social beings. And then the book stops. But the path is open for us to move further in this direction.

The present work situates itself in this larger field, of which a few main lines have been sketched, as they appeared at the time of composition. My book may be seen as an extension of the attempts just mentioned but inspired too by both Sveinsson and by the Romantic Hauch's determination not simply to perceive the sagas as works of art, but to take them seriously as such, which is to say to read them on the supposition that they contain not a truth about their fictive subject, but rather a truth of another kind, the truth about the conceptual universe with which the people of the thirteenth century met their challenges, the truth about the philosophy they established in order to manage their lives.

The present work distinguishes itself of course from the historical school which became history a long time ago, and also from the Icelandic School by virtue of its attempt to seek out basic patterns common to a number of sagas and to relate these to an overall notion of the basic forces in the conditions to which saga literature was a response. It differs furthermore from the European School by not paying any attention to possible models in continental literature and in continental medieval Christendom, but by concentrating on the sagas as integrated works of art with internal structures, and on the societal conditions by which they were shaped. The study at hand is related to the Norwegian School in that it seeks answers to psychological questions, but differs crucially from this school in not seeking a real person behind the fictional character in the work, but rather the total statement of the work of art of which the characters are parts. And finally it differs from the works of the Ethical-Aesthetic School partly by taking the individual work's artistic unity as the fundamental datum and by seeing the work in a historical context, in a particular place within a particular historical sequence of events.

It has been the basic idea in the preceding chapters that if we want to understand the sagas as works of literary fiction in an historical context, we cannot avoid first using all the tools of literary analysis on them in order to discover the statement made by each work. It is this statement and not any single part of the work that can be set in relation to a world beyond the work.

But doing so is also necessary if the sagas are not simply to be admired as a timeless revelation or catalogued as a mechanical result of influences, but read and understood as a human answer to the challenges of existence at a particular place and a particular time. That takes a conception of the world beyond the works. That world too is perceived in wholes and not as the sum of a number of episodes.

SELECT BIBLIOGRAPHY

Allen, Richard F. *Fire and Iron. Critical Approaches to* Njáls Saga. Pittsburgh: University of Pittsburgh Press, 1971.

Andersson, Theodore, M. *The Icelandic Family Saga. An Analytic Reading*. Harvard Studies in Comparative Literature 28. Cambridge, Mass.: Harvard University Press, 1967.

---. *The Problem of Icelandic Saga Origins. A Historical Survey*. Yale Germanic Studies 1. New Haven and London: Yale University Press, 1964.

---. "Some Ambiguities in *Gísla Saga*. A Balance Sheet," *Bibliography of Old Norse-Icelandic Studies*, pp. 7-42. Copenhagen, 1969.

Andersson, Theodore, M. and William Ian Miller. *Law and Literature in Medieval Iceland*. Ljósvetninga saga *and* Valla-Ljóts saga. Stanford: Stanford University Press, 1989.

Baetke, Walter. *Christliches Lehngut in der Sagareligion*. Berichte über die Verhandl. der sächsischen Akademie der Wissenschaften zu Leipzig, Philol.-hist. Klasse, Bd. 98, Heft 6. Berlin, 1952.

---. *Über die Entstehung der Isländersagas*. Berichte über die Verhandl. der sächsischen Akademie der Wissenschaften zu Leipzig, Philol.-hist. Klasse, Bd. 102, Heft 5. Berlin: Akademie-Verlag, 1956.

Bley, A. *Eigla-Studien*. Gand: Van Goethem, 1909.

Brøndsted, Mogens. *Digtning og skæbne. En studie i æstetisk determination*. Copenhagen: Munksgaard, 1958.

Bååth, A.U. *Studier öfver kompositionen i några isländska ättsagor*. Lund: F. Berlings boktr. og stilgjuteri, 1885.

Byock, Jesse L. *Feud in the Icelandic Saga*. Berkeley, Los Angeles, and London: University of California Press, 1982.

---. *Medieval Iceland. Society, Sagas, and Power*. Berkeley, Los Angeles, and London: University of California Press, 1988.

Clover, Carol J. *The Medieval Saga*. Ithaca and London: Cornell University Press, 1982.

Clover, Carol J. and John Lindow, eds. *Old Norse-Icelandic Literature: A Critical Guide*. Islandica 45. Ithaca and London: Cornell University Press, 1985.

Einarsson, Bjarni. *Skáldasögur. Um uppruna og edli ástaskáldasagnanna fornu*. Reykjavík: Bókaútgáfa Menningarsjóds, 1961.

Gudmundsson, Bardi. *Höfundur Njálu*. Reykjavík: Bókaútgáfa Menningarsjóds, 1958.

Haeckel, Margarete. *Die Darstellung und Funktion des Traumes in der isländischen Familiensaga*. Hamburg: H. Proctor, 1934.

Hallberg, Peter. *The Icelandic Saga (Den isländska sagan*, 1956). Trans. Paul Schack. Lincoln, Neb.: University of Nebraska Press, 1962.
Halleux, Pierre. *Aspects littéraires de la Saga de Hrafnkel*. Paris: Société d'edition "Les Belles Lettres," 1963.
Helgason, Jón. *Norrøn Litteraturhistorie*. Copenhagen: Levin og Munksgaard, 1934.
Heller, Rolf. "Studien zu Aufbau und Stil der Laxdœla Saga," *Arkiv för Nordisk Filologi* 75, 113-67. Lund, 1960.
Hollander, Lee M. "The Structure of *Eyrbyggja saga*," *Journal of English and Germanic Philology* 58, 222-27. 1959
Holtsmark, Anne. *Studies in the Gisla Saga*. Studia Norvegica 6. Oslo: Aschehoug, 1951.
Jeffrey, Margaret. *The Discourse in Seven Icelandic Sagas*. Bryn Mawr, Pa., 1934.
Jóhannesson, Jón, Magnús Finnbogason and Kristján Eldjárn, eds. *Sturlunga saga* I-II. Reykjavík: Sturlunguútgáfan, 1946.
Jónsson, Finnur. *Norsk-islendske kultur- og sprogforhold i 9. og 10. Årh*. Copenhagen: A. F. Host, 1921.
---. *Den oldnorske og oldislandske Litteraturs Historie*, II. Copenhagen: G. E. C. Gad, 1898; 2 ed. 1923.
Ker, W.P. *Epic and Romance. Essays on Medieval Literature*. London: Macmillan, 1896. Reprinted, New York: Dover Publications, 1957.
Kinck, Hans E. *Mange slags kunst*. Kristiania, 1921. Reprinted (revised), *Sagaenes ånd og skikkelser*. Oslo: Aschehoug, 1951. (Includes „Et par ting om ættesagaen. Skikkelser den ikke forstod", first printed in 1916, and „Kjærligheten I Kormaks saga", first printed in 1918.)
Larsen, Martin. "Introduktion" in *Njal og branden på Bergtorshvol*, Dansklærerforeningen, 2 ed., pp. 165-229. Copenhagen: Gyldendal, 1965.
Lie, Hallvard. "Noen metodologiske overveielser i anledning av et bind af 'Íslenzk fornrit'," *Maal og Minne*, pp. 97-138. Oslo, 1939.
---. "Jorvikferden. Et Vendepunkt i Egil Skallagrimssons Liv," *Edda: Nordisk tidsskrift for litteraturforskning*, pp. 145-248. Oslo: Universitetsforlaget, 1946.
Liestøl, Knut. *Upphavet til den islendske ættesaga*. Oslo: Aschehoug, 1929.
Lönnroth, Lars. *European Sources of Icelandic Saga-Writing. An Essay Based on Previous Studies*. Stockholm: Boktryckeri Aktiebolaget Thule, 1965.
---. *Njáls Saga. A Critical Introduction*. Berkeley, Los Angeles, and London: University of California Press, 1976.
Ludwig, Werner. *Untersuchungen über den Entwicklungsgang und die Funktion des Dialogs in der isländischen Saga*. Gräfenhainichen: A. Heine, 1934.
Meulengracht Sørensen, Preben. *Fortælling og ære. Studier i islændingesagaerne*. Aarhus: Aarhus University Press, 1993a.
---. *Saga and Society (Saga og Samfund, 1977)*. Trans. John Tucker. Odense: Odense University Press, 1993b.
Miller, William Ian. *Bloodtaking and Peacemaking: Feud, Law and Society in Saga Iceland*. Chicago and London: University of Chicago Press, 1990.

Nordal, Sigurður. *The Historical Element in the Icelandic Family Sagas*, W.P. Ker Memorial Lecture 15. Glasgow: Jackson, Son and Co., 1957.

---. *Hrafnkels Saga Freysgoða. (Hrafnkatla,* 1940). Trans. R.G. Thomas. Cardiff: University of Wales Press, 1958.

---. "Sagalitteraturen," *Litteraturhistorie B: Norge og Island.* Nordisk Kultur, 8B, pp. 180-273. Stockholm: Bonnier, 1953.

Norrøn Fortællekunst. Hans Bekker-Nielsen, Thorkil Damsgaard Olsen, Ole Widding. Copenhagen: Akademisk forlag, 1965.

Olgeirsson, Einar. *Ættasamfélag og ríkisvald í þjóðveldi Íslendinga.* Reykjavík: Heimskringla, 1954

Paasche, Frederik. "Tendens og syn i kongesagaen," *Edda: Nordisk tidsskrift for litteraturforskning* 17, pp. 1-17. Kristiania, 1922.

Pálsson, Hermann. *Art and Ethics in Hrafnkel's Saga.* Copenhagen: Munksgaard, 1971.

---. *Hrafnkels saga og Freysgydlingar.* Reykjavík: Thjódsaga, 1962.

---. *Siðfræði Hrafnkels sögu.* Reykjavík: Heimskringla, 1966.

Petersen, N. M. *Bidrag til den oldnordiske Literaturs Historie.* Copenhagen: Berlingske Bogtrykkeri, 1866.

Prinz, Reinhard. *Die Schöpfung der Gísla Saga Súrssonar, Ein Beitrag zur Entstehungsgeschichte der isländischen Saga.* Breslau: F. Hirt, 1935.

Rubow, Paul V. "Den islandske Familieroman," *Tilskueren* 45/1, 347-57, 1928. Reprinted in his *Små kritiske breve.* Copenhagen: Gyldendal, 1936.

---. "Den Islandske sagalitteratur i nutiden," *Tilskueren* 45/2, 170-74, 1928. Reprinted in his *Små kritiske breve.* Copenhagen: Gyldendal, 1936.

Schomerus, Rudolf. *Die Religion der Nordgermanen im Spiegel christlicher Darstellung.* Göttingen: F. Noske, 1936.

Seewald, Franz. *Die Saga von Gisli Surssön.* Göttingen, 1934. Reprinted Stuttgart: Reclam, 1976.

Steblin-Kamenskij, M.I. "An Attempt at a Semantic Approach to the Problem of Authorship in Old Icelandic Literature," *Arkiv för Nordisk Filologi* 81, 24-34. Lund, 1966.

---. *The Saga Mind* (*Mir saga,* 1971). Trans. Kenneth H. Ober. Odense: Odense University Press, 1973.

Sveinsson, Einar Ólafur. *Á Njálsbuð.* Reykjavik, 1943.

---. *The Age of the Sturlungs. Icelandic Civilization in the Thirteenth Century.* Islandica 36. (*Sturlungaöld,* 1940). Trans. Jóhann S. Hannesson. Ithaca: Cornell University Press, 1953.

---. "Njáls saga", *Scipta Islandica* I, 5-30, Stockholm 1950.

---. *Dating the Icelandic Sagas. An essay in Method.* London: Viking Society for Northern Research, 1958.

---. "The Icelandic Family Sagas and the Period in which their Authors Lived" *Acta Philologica Scandinavica* 12, 71-90. Copenhagen, 1938.

Thomas, R.G. "The Sturlung Age as an Age of Saga Writing," *The Germanic Review* 25, 50-66. New York, 1950.
Toorn, M. C. van den. *Ethics and Moral in Icelandic Saga Literature*. Assen: Van Gorcum & Comp., 1955.
Tucker, John. "George Johnston's *The Saga of Gisli*." *Malahat Review* 87, 83-91. Victoria, 1987.
---. ed. *Sagas of the Icelanders: A Book of Essays*. New York: Garland Publishing, 1989
Turville-Petre, Gabriel. "Gísli Súrsson and his Poetry. Traditions and Influences," *Modern Language Review* 39, 374-91. London, 1944.
---. *Origins of Icelandic Literature*. Oxford: Clarendon Press, 1953.
Tveitane, Mattias. "Europeisk påvirkning på den norrøne sagalitteraturen. Noen synspunkter," *Edda: Nordisk tidsskrift for litteraturforskning*, pp. 73-95, Oslo: Universitetsforlaget, 1969.

POSTSCRIPT TO THE ENGLISH EDITION

1

Saga scholarship has been augmented by many books and articles in the thirty years that have passed since this book appeared in Danish. But no dramatic paradigm shift has occurred. The dominant models that govern the questions we put to the material are those that were asked at that time – with one important exception, a book that came out in Russian the same year that *Kaos og Kærlighed* was published. Had I known it – or had I possessed the knowledge I subsequently gained from it – I could have formulated my thoughts more clearly on a decisive point.

I do not mean to imply by this that no other new knowledge about the sagas of Icelanders has been produced, far from it. But the answers proposed are to questions quite different from those raised in *Kaos og Kærlighed*. There is a discernible tendency to return to the view that the sagas of Icelanders are factual historical documents; see, for example, William Ian Miller's *Bloodtaking and Peacemaking: Feud, Law, and Society in Saga Iceland* (1990). Otherwise two schools in particular have dominated scholarship: the one that I referred to above as the European School, in other words the approach that searches for influences from contemporary or earlier European literature; and the Oral-Formulaic School that builds on a moderate version of the free-prose theory, specifically on the assumption that the material that entered the sagas must have been formed by the oral tradition in the same way – in other words out of formulae of the same kind – as one can observe among the oral narrators who have continued to flourish as late as the twentieth century in the Balkans and who could therefore be studied in the field.

The Oral-Formulaic School and the European School have both been most active in the United States. Taken as a whole, in the last few decades American scholars have been the most diligent students of the sagas. The two schools share a common feature: they favour dividing the individual saga up into segments or *þættir*, in order to see how the individual *þáttr* might be traced back to either a written or an oral source, to an influence or a loan. So they share a tacit assumption

– the inheritance of Romanticism – that a phenomenon can best be understood if its origins are understood. They refrain from considering the whole saga as a completed structure. They are more interested in knowing how it came into existence, than in what it is that exists. The sagas of Icelanders continue to exercise the same attraction as in earlier times for researchers with philological, folkloristic, historical and similar interests, but relatively less for scholars with literary sensitivity and experience.

A useful survey of this scholarship is found in *Old Norse-Icelandic Literature: A Critical Guide* (1985), edited by Carol J. Clover and John Lindow, which contains refreshingly subjective critical commentaries on individual works. Among these may be found some of the critical reactions that *Kaos og Kærlighed* originally elicited (258f), including those of Clover herself.

2

The best source for what has happened in recent saga scholarship is Preben Meulengracht Sørensen's *Fortælling og Ære: Studier i Islændingersagaer* (1993a), which contains a meticulous bibliography and whose argument addresses itself to many of the works listed. This is however not the most important thing about the study. I include it, as one of only four titles mentioned in this Postscript, because it is a comprehensive and substantive work which moreover distinguishes itself by its principal interest, the literary dimension of the sagas.

It is Meulengracht Sørensen's perception that the code of honour is decisive in the determination of the saga's narrative form. He argues this position by means of – among other things – the analysis of a number of complete sagas, for "the literary analysis is a precondition of the historiographical" (23), a conviction which he maintains in noteworthy opposition to many – in fact, most – of his predecessors.

The position produces important new observations about the sagas' use of the technical device specialists in epic theory call "the narrator" or the "point of view" (63-78). This leads also to a fine description of the society in which the code of honour can become so decisive, the stateless society without any official police force, in which everyone was his brother's keeper. Meulengracht Sørensen describes this medieval version of a Stasi-society as follows:

> Icelandic society was what ethnographers call a "face to face" society. It was made up of small social units whose members knew each other and could look one another in the eye, and where everybody was therefore continually under scrutiny. This held true in the farm household, in thing assemblies and on shipboard during voyages. The whole society belonged to the public sphere. In the life of the individual only a few things could be kept secret from others, because the private sphere in the modern sense did not exist. House design, with common living and sleeping rooms, ensured that all activities were open to everyone. . . . The composition of the household, with serving people who moved on moving days, made it difficult to keep secrets from one's neighbours. Guests and travellers were a source of observation and news as in *Njal's Saga*, in which begging women carry gossip between Hlidarendi and Bergthorshvol. This example shows one of the negative sides of this sharing of opinion and information, but openness and stories about others were a necessary institution in a society which depended upon everyone knowing a good deal about everyone else. Public opinion became an important yardstick and an efficient corrective *vis-à-vis* the behaviour of the individual. (208)

The description of this medieval Icelandic society is a good occasion to call to mind just what kind of "Love" is intended by the title to the present work and the analysis that it presents: not the romantic feeling experienced by the individual, which is almost unknown in the sagas, but the behaviour that follows its own instincts regardless of social norms or public scandal. That is what sets in motion social chaos.

No, says Meulengracht Sørensen, not the erotic drive but the revenge imperative is what drives saga narrative: "Only through revenge and counter-revenge are honour and status brought into equilibrium again. That is the lesson of the sagas" (246). Is it really? I ask. To my way of thinking the reverse is true. In saga after saga, as the preceding account shows, this balance sheet based on honour goes haywire. The more murders committed to rectify the balance and restore order, the worse becomes the social chaos brought about by the killing.

Only three pages later we find Meulengracht Sørensen deriving a contrary lesson from the sagas, namely that the ideal man, possessed of all the qualities that the sagas value highly, ends up suffering "crisis, tragic death or defeat" (249), despite these excellent qualities. Why? On account of something he calls the "forces of chaos" (259) but which he fails to spell out. I am in agreement with him. My book begins, one might say, where his ends. It is an attempt to put a name to some of the "forces of chaos" that the sagas of Icelanders depict.

3

But truth then, what of it? What exactly was the relationship that existed between the Icelandic saga and the reality it told of? Meulengracht Sørensen rejects both the classic answers. The sagas are neither history nor historical romances, but apparently both by turns: "we may read them as the statement of a reality that becomes both historical and poetic, when it is set down in writing" (24). What precisely this means, i.e. what is supposed to happen when the event is put in writing, is not clear to me.

What it *might* mean lies at the heart of the most original book to be written about the sagas for a long time, the Russian scholar M.I. Steblin-Kamenskij's *Mir Saga* (1971), meaning "the saga's universe," published in English translation as *The Saga Mind* (1973). Steblin-Kamenskij is not content to say both-and. He defines two conceptions of truth that he then sets aside, historical truth and artistic truth, and goes on to name a third to replace them which he calls "syncretic truth."

By historical truth Steblin-Kamenskij understands "the exact report of what has occurred," by artistic truth "a vivid and living idea of the reality of the past" (22). The Icelanders of old had only one conception of truth, "syncretic truth": "Whoever reported syncretic truth about the past strove simultaneously for accuracy and for reproduction of reality in all its living fullness" (24).

Medieval Icelanders had no concept of fiction, according to him. Hence the irresolvable dispute between book-prose and free-prose, saga scholars' never ending – because endless – game of Truth-or-Consequences. This was the obstacle that I was trying to circumvent by taking as my starting point Hauch's assertion that an "artistic design" can be found in the sagas. The choice between the two words that were available, history and art, was thus decided in favour of the latter. Had I known the Russian scholar's third concept, I might have adopted his argumentation, perhaps also his words.

It would have been better than to use the word art – in any event at the time. But perhaps Steblin-Kamenskij's formulation has become less necessary today. He wrote:

> "For the modern man everything told of the past is of necessity either historical truth or artistic truth. It is therefore very difficult for him to imagine truth which is neither the one nor the other, nor anything in between" (32).

Yes, perhaps it is. But what has happened to "the modern man" in the meantime is that "he" has become postmodern, i.e. not only able to conceive of something between "artistic truth" and "historical truth," but rather unable to imagine anything that is not a mixture of the two. Docudrama, new journalism, faction, new historicism, deconstruction – a series of mixed forms and sceptical research strategies have opened the alert reader's eyes to the discovery that art shapes reality, and that reality assumes the shape of narrative, even in scholarship. The sharp division between the scholarly *wie es eigentlich gewesen* and the artistic interpretation has become ever more difficult to maintain. It is no longer the Middle Age's "syncretic truth" that looks like a rare exception, but rather the post-Romantic, positivistic conception of truth, which after all has dominated the humanities only for a century.

One consequence of Steblin-Kamenskij's having written during the hundred years dominated by positivism is his notably narrow definition of "artistic truth." For it is indeed not the commonly held understanding that he espouses when he defines artistic truth as "a vivid and living idea of the reality of the past." Rather this is a watering down – or, if you will, an enrichment – of positivistic scholarship's historical truth, the so-called referential concept of truth, which forms part of the *correspondence-theory* of truth. By artistic truth most people understand something that has very little to do with referential truth, i.e. with factual correspondence. In a modern context "artistic truth" in prose is rather the narrative's refusal of compromise and rejection of deceit, its inner consistency, something comparable to what epistemology calls the *coherence-theory* of truth.

In any event this was the kind of truth I sought three decades ago, urged on by the sense that it is to be found in the sagas of Icelanders, from which it can be extracted in the form of an inherent "conception of life," or a conceptual universe, a coherent understanding of the forces at work in the world, of what should be avoided and what striven for. In other words, these texts embody a philosophy: an understanding of what *should* be, together with the description of what *is*.

Here is a feature of *Kaos og Kærlighed*, which shows that its roots do not lie in postmodernism – whose tenets converge with those of this book in one point only, the postmodernist deconstruction of the concept of art by means of an extended concept of the text. No, the book is rooted in older patterns of thought, so far as I can see basically in the Enlightenment, specifically its notion that it is not merely the single saga that can be read as a coherent whole, but the whole genre that can be read as a Grand Narrative – and furthermore that from this Grand Narrative an Icelandic myth emerges, which has the function of making the individual freer to understand and deal with his own time.

Steblin-Kamenskij's brilliance consisted in his knack for pointing out the words that Icelanders used to denominate all the central concepts of the various areas of their lives – on the reasonable assumption that they did not think thoughts for which they lacked words. It is by this procedure that he arrived at the conclusion that they did not possess any concept of fiction.

With this knowledge in hand using the word art to refer to one of the Icelanders' most important products seems questionable, given how narrowly the conceptions of art and fiction are conjoined in our minds. When today I once again present my reflections from a former time for discussion, it is because what Steblin-Kamenskij chose to call "syncretic truth" is consistent with them. Despite my use of the word art in the analyses, as I said in my Preface, these are "independent of either theory in the debate," i.e. the two theories which are bound up with the definitions of art (book-prose theory) and history (free-prose theory) respectively. Or, to quote the phrasing of my last chapter: "Today it is once again possible to see the kinship between history and poetry and fiction, not in the romantic way as revelations of Truth, but as different expressions of the truth about how people in a particular time have interpreted their circumstances – with the help of fiction, that is 'poetry,' or by means of the selection and ordering of the facts about the past, that is 'history.'"

Here a perspective opens up on a fourth concept of the truth, neither the artistic nor the historical nor a fusion of the two, "syncretic truth," but the truth about life *as it functioned* for the people who in thirteenth-century Iceland wrote and read and listened to and told the sagas of Icelanders as we know them from the manuscripts, irrespective of the origin of the bits and pieces of which they are composed, and irrespective of how they relate to the reality of the tenth and eleventh centuries which they purport to represent. This conception is related to, if not identical with, what epistemology calls the *pragmatic theory* of truth.

Steblin-Kamenskij's delineation of the saga's universe with the help of etymology is a useful opportunity to underline Christianity's role in these works. As I have analysed it in this book, Christianity is often the bearer of a "happy ending," in the form of the "hoped-for Christian society of mercy." This might suggest the idea that Christianity spread throughout Iceland because it brought mercy. Wrong, says Steblin-Kamenskij in *The Saga Mind*, and rightly so. Christianity made headway because Icelanders were convinced that its God was stronger than their gods. The commandment it introduced was not "Thou shalt not kill," but "Thou shalt not kill thine enemies, only those of God and the king" (113). That the right to kill passed from the individual to the state did not mean that the murder rate dropped.

This view, however, does not challenge the reality of Christianity's role in the sagas of Icelanders. It is always the expectation of mercifulness that is the necessary final link in the structure of the Icelandic myth. Which generally speaking is a good indicator that it was in the hands of Christian writers that the sagas of Icelanders achieved the final forms in which we know them.

When I today read *Chaos and Love*, it strikes me that it is as a contribution to this, the functional "truth" in the sagas of Icelanders, that the book can best be read. What I miss in it is not an account of the relationship between the sagas' literary sources, their historical subject matter or their oral pre-histories; others have attended to these tasks. What I miss most is the substantiation of the thematic analyses by means of a fundamental exploration of the forms in which the themes achieve expression, i.e. the analysis of rhetorical and narrative forms in the sagas from the point of view of function rather than origins. Too little of this is found in this book, more in Hallberg and Meulengracht Sørensen, but the last named is right when he maintains (76) that a comprehensive investigation of this question is still lacking.

Thus there are tasks enough to take up for anyone who wants to have a go at the sagas of Icelanders. What characterises these narrative works of art – and works of art is still the most precise designation for them – is and remains the fact that the more one reads them, the more new secrets they reveal.

4

Saga scholarship also has two concepts of truth or relevance, a philological-folkloristic-historical one and a literary one. Individuals like Meulengracht Sørensen have attempted to create a syncretism between them, but the prospects of succeeding in uniting the two cultures are not great.

When I had completed the manuscript to this book, with some trepidation I asked my former teacher of Old Icelandic, Jón Helgason, the master of Nordic philology, to read it through. He did so and proposed a number of corrections, which I incorporated. He offered only one summary comment on the work – with praise and blame he was for the most part as taciturn and indirect as his countrymen, the saga-writers.

– You seem rather to belong to the Hauch-Rubow tradition.

The observation was hardly meant as praise. Nevertheless I remember that I blushed and thought to myself that it was almost too high praise. I still think so. At the same time I hope that he was not entirely wrong, for it is the works of this tradition that have taught me the most about the issues that in my opinion matter in the sagas of Icelanders.

The University of Copenhagen, 2001

Thomas Bredsdorff